The Rainmaker's Friend

James Chalmers

For Andrew, Ben and John

The Rainmaker's Friend

James Chalmers

Irene Howat

CHRISTIAN FOCUS

Copyright © 2006 Christian Focus Publications
ISBN 1-84550-154-3
978-1-84550-154-9

Published by
Christian Focus Publications
Geanies House, Fearn, Tain, Ross-shire
IV20 1TW, Scotland
United Kingdom
www.christianfocus.com
email: info@ christianfocus.com

Cover design by Danie van Straaten
Cover illustration Neil Reed
Printed and bound in Denmark
by Nørhaven Paperback A/S

Contents

River rescue

James stretched his back hard against the measuring rod that was nailed to the kitchen wall and stood as straight and tall as he possibly could.

'Will you put a mark on the rod to show my height?' he asked his mother. 'I must have grown since last year.'

Mrs Chalmers marked her son's height carefully and James turned round to see if there was a difference between the line made on August 4th 1850 and the one made today, August 4th 1851, his tenth birthday.

'Look at that!' he laughed. 'I've grown a lot. Before long I'll be as tall as Dad.'

'James thinks he's the tallest ten-year-old in Scotland,' his sister teased.

'Sisters!' thought James crossly. 'I wonder if anyone wants two sisters. They could have mine free.'

That afternoon, when the day's schooling was over, James and his friends sat on the banks of the stream that rushed down the hillside near their school.

'Ten's quite old,' said Calum. 'A lot can happen to a person in ten years.'

'Both good and bad,' agreed James.

'What's the best thing that's happened to you in your ten years?' Dugald asked.

James thought for a while before answering.

'I think it was when I tried to build a boat with my

friends in Ardrishaig. It was such hard work! We decided to tar a herring-box to make it waterproof. As I was captain I had the first sail in it. I climbed into the box and my friends tied a long line to it and dragged it into the sea. At first it seemed as though it would sink under my weight, but it didn't! A big wave lifted it, and I was up, up and away! The current caught me and, for just a few minutes, I felt like the captain of a great clipper. With the wind in my face and the herring-box caught in the current it seemed as though there was nothing between me and a life on the ocean wave.'

Dugald looked at his friend's excited face.

'What happened then?' he asked. 'How far did you go?'

James shook his head then laughed sheepishly.

'Too far,' he said. 'The current washed me out into Loch Fyne. It took some strong swimmers to save me from drowning ... or reaching the open sea.'

'Think of it,' Calum commented. 'You might have ended up being washed ashore on the South Sea Islands! But what's the worst thing that's ever happened to you?'

James Chalmers knew the answer to that question without giving it a second thought.

'Once, in my last school, an older boy said he'd give me sweets if I'd chew something else first.'

'You'd agree to that,' Dugald laughed, 'for there's nothing you like better than sweets.'

'I did,' James admitted. 'The boy gave me a twist of tobacco. I chewed the stuff for all I was worth because he was standing there watching. When the teacher called us in for lessons I could hardly get to the school. I felt so sick and my legs just wanted to give way under me.'

'Did you get your sweets?' asked Calum.

'I've not finished the story,' James said. 'There was worse still to come.'

His friends sat silent, wondering what could be worse than that.

'My legs gave way just as I arrived at the classroom door and the teacher had to lift me up and carry me in.'

'That must have been embarrassing!' whistled Calum.

'Not half as embarrassing as what happened next. When the teacher heard that I'd been chewing tobacco he made me sit on his high chair with a tall chimneypot hat on my head!'

'What did the class do?' asked Dugald.

'I've no idea,' James admitted. 'The teacher's head was so much bigger than mine that his hat slid over my ears and landed, plonk, on my shoulders. It left me in total darkness!'

'Phew!' Calum said. 'I'm glad nothing like that has ever happened to me. I don't think I could face looking at people ever again!'

'Do you want to know the most embarrassing thing that's ever happened to me?' asked Dugald.

Pleased to think about something other than his early encounter with tobacco, James sat back against a tree stump to listen to his friend.

'When I was six I caught whooping cough. Mum was worried about me because I was coughing fit to burst, so she took me to the two old women in Inveraray who said they had a cure. You'll never guess what their cure was. They got a donkey. One stood on one side and one on the other and they passed me between its legs and over its back!'

'That was a cure for whooping cough?' asked an amazed James. 'Did it work?'

'Don't be silly!' Calum laughed. 'That's just superstitious nonsense. It's just as silly as the superstition that if you hear a dog crying there's sure to have been a death.'

'My dog cries when she's tied up outside,' said James. 'And if someone died every time she cried, there'd be nobody left alive in Inveraray.'

One day Mr John McArthur, schoolmaster, was aware of some unrest in Glenaray School during the lunchtime interval.

'What's going on, boys?' he asked, when he went out with the handbell to tell them that it was time for lessons to begin.

'Nothing, Sir,' all the boys said in unison.

'If I'm not mistaken there's mischief afoot,' said the teacher severely. 'Why else are you divided up into two groups, with those from the town on one side and those from Glenaray on the other?'

The boys all looked down at their feet. It was a constant source of surprise to them that Mr McArthur seemed to be able to read their minds.

After school that afternoon the boys broke into two groups again: *The Townies* and *The Glenies*. Instead of going home by their usual Three Bridges route, they headed for the high road towards Kilmun. That was a good place for fighting where they were unlikely to be disturbed. Suddenly a clod of earth flew through the air and hit a Townie slap on the back. He spun round, picked up a stone and threw it at the boy he thought had attacked him. Before long missiles zipped in all directions and fists flew. James was not the only one to head for home with a bleeding nose and a black eye. But now that the air was cleared *The Townies* and *The Glenies* could live at peace for another six weeks or so before battle commenced yet again.

Some months later the area around Inveraray had heavy rain all morning. But, as the afternoon wore on, the rain stopped and the sun came out.

'You'll get home dry,' said Mr McArthur, opening the classroom door at the end of the school day. 'But watch where you put your feet for some of the puddles are far deeper than your boots!'

'Look at the torrent!' whistled James, as they walked the short distance along the River Aray.

'All the streams flowing into it are full,' Dugald observed. 'I wonder if the Aray will burst her banks before the night's out.'

'Doubt it,' Calum thought aloud. 'The rain's stopped now. The water level will begin to go down soon.'

A short distance away another group of children was nearing the Three Bridges. Something strange was happening up ahead. James stopped to take a closer look and then he heard a scream rip through the air.

'Help!'

James broke into a run before his mind had time to even wonder what was wrong. Where floodwater was concerned you ran first and thought second.

'Johnnie's in the Aray!' someone yelled.

James took in the scene in an instant. Hauling off his jacket, he dashed for the new wooden bridge, scrambled underneath and grabbed on to it for support. He then stretched as far as he could underneath it to catch Johnnie as the torrent rushed him through. Suddenly his arm was hit by the weight of the boy and he grabbed for his clothes. Against all probability James managed to catch Johnnie's coat.

'I can't hang on any longer!' he thought desperately.

Then, in a flash of inspiration, he knew just exactly what to do. He released his hold on the bridge and allowed himself and Johnnie to be washed a little way along the Aray to where they could more easily get out.

'Grab that branch!' Dugald yelled from the riverside.

James looked to where his friend was pointing and saw a low branch of willow hanging down to the water. As he and Johnnie were being swept past it, James grabbed with his left hand, while still hanging on to the half-drowned young boy with the other. Suddenly everything happened at once and everyone spoke at the same time.

'Is Johnnie dead?'

'You did it!'

'That was amazing!'

'What a catch!'

Hands reached out to the boys from all directions and both were hauled out of the River Aray on to the bank where Johnnie was laid on his front and thumped on the back to force the water from his lungs. The best noise James heard that day was the rasping cough that showed that Johnnie was still alive. It was several days before Johnnie was back at school. But James, the young hero, was there basking in the glory of having saved his school friend's life.

The rain came back that evening and continued for days. Sunday morning dawned grey and wet, as had Saturday, as had Friday.

'I'm glad I'm a girl,' said one of James's sisters. 'Girls don't have to go to church when it's pouring rain.'

'Some do,' James replied. 'It's just because it's such a

long walk that Dad doesn't insist on you going when the weather's as bad as this.'

'Dad,' said James, as they walked through the drizzle to church. 'Can I go to Mr Meikle's Sunday School? That's where my friends go and I'd like to go with them.'

'Mr Meikle's a fine man,' said his father. 'I'll think about the Sunday School and tell you when I've made up my mind.'

James knew not to pursue the subject. His father was a quiet man. He didn't say much, but when he did speak he said what he meant and rarely changed his mind.

'Let me hear you saying the 23rd Psalm,' said Mr Chalmers, when they had about a mile still to go.

James said the psalm from beginning to end without a single mistake.

'You've remembered it well,' commented his father. 'And I hope you believe it too.'

'Do you remember when we lived in Ardrishaig?' James asked his father. 'You once gave me a sixpenny piece for learning the 23rd Psalm from the Bible.'

'I remember that,' said James's father.

'Well,' went on the boy. 'I'd never had a six pence before that. So I gave it to Mum and she gave me a penny to spend and kept the rest to put into her housekeeping money.'

'I never knew that,' smiled Mr Chalmers. 'Now, let's say the 23rd Psalm together.'

The autumn and winter storms did some damage to the stonework of Inveraray Jail, and James's father, being a stonemason, was asked to make the repairs.

'I could do with some help with the job,' he told his

young son. 'Would you be willing to work for me on Saturdays until the job's done?'

'Yes,' agreed James, but not too quickly. Saturdays were sometimes spent down at the quay on the local fishing boats and repointing the jail's stonework seemed a poor alternative. But there were always interesting things to be seen at the jail, as James knew from past experience.

'Hello, young man,' said one of the men who worked at Inveraray jail, when he saw him labouring for his father. 'There's no rest for you this Saturday. But I tell you what, when your dad gives you a break come into the office and I'll show you some things that will interest you.'

James grinned from ear to ear. 'Maybe this isn't going to be so dull after all,' he thought, as he began work once again.

After several hours of hard toil Mr Chalmers sat down to drink his bottle of cold tea and James headed in the direction of the office. When he arrived there were papers everywhere, some of them yellow with age.

'Look at this,' the man said. 'I've been reading through the jail records and I thought you might be interested in seeing some of the earlier ones.'

James looked at the long lists of names, crimes and punishments.

'Ishabel Campbell, aged 12, for the theft of bread, four weeks in jail.

Jeanie Campbell, aged 34, widow, mother of Ishabel, for the theft of bread, six months in jail.

Norman Morrison, aged 45, for drunken and disorderly conduct, one month in jail.

John Macdonald, aged 39, for the theft of a year-old sheep, transported to the colonies.'

'Do you think Ishabel and her mother were starving when they stole the bread?' James asked the jailor.

'I suppose they might have been,' the man agreed. 'Especially as it says her mother was a widow woman.'

'It must have been awful to be transported to the colonies. Imagine being sent to the other side of the world just for stealing a sheep.'

That evening, after a hard day's work had been done on the jail's stonework, Mr Chalmers and James set off on their long walk home. As usual his father was not very talkative and much of the time the boy was left with his own thoughts for company.

'I suppose it might have been quite exciting to be sent to the colonies. I wonder if John Macdonald thought it was an adventure or a punishment. I imagine it depended on whether or not he had a wife and children.'

As they walked up Glenaray, James thought of the long journey from Inverary in the west of Scotland to the Australian colonies. Holding a picture of the world in his mind, he traced a mental line down Loch Fyne and into the Firth of Clyde, from there out to the Atlantic Ocean and south, over the equator and into the Indian Ocean before turning east towards Australia.

'It's an awful long way,' he thought aloud.

'There's no need to complain about it,' said Mr Chalmers, thinking James was talking of the walk between Inveraray and their home up the glen. 'I'll be walking it every day for several weeks to finish the work on the jail.'

15

James reckoned that his father would not think of transportation to the penal colonies as an adventure so he kept his thoughts to himself.

Any excuse to leave school

'I've thought about what you were saying,' Mr Chalmers told James a week or two later. 'You can go to Mr Meikle's Sunday School with your friends. You'll come to no harm there. And that's not the only new place you'll be going.'

'What do you mean?' the boy asked.

'We're moving from this house to one away up on the hillside,' explained his father. 'It's not that far.'

James scowled. 'It's not that near either,' he thought, but he knew better than to say it aloud.

Some months later, after James was well settled in his new Sunday School, he decided that he didn't want to go after all and took a Sunday off.

'Hello, Minister,' said a surprised Mr Chalmers, when they met on the road four miles from Inveraray. 'You're a long way from home today. You'll be out visiting, I've no doubt.'

'I was actually making my way up the hill to your house,' Mr Meikle explained. 'James wasn't in Sunday School last week and I thought I'd see what was wrong with him. He's not ill, I hope.'

'No,' said Mr Chalmers. 'He's not ill. And he'll not be causing you any more long walks to check on his health. James'll be at Sunday School next Sunday and every one after that too.'

'I'm glad I met you then,' said the minister.

The two men talked for a while before Mr Meikle turned back towards Inveraray and the stonemason headed for home.

James's father spoke seriously to him that evening, and he was left in no doubt where he was to be each Sunday.

'You'll not be absent again without good reason,' the boy was told. 'We can't have that good man wasting his time checking on your health when there's nothing whatever the matter with you!'

In the darkness that night, before they fell asleep, both father and son thought about the very same thing. Both knew that only a good man would bother to walk miles to check why a young lad was not at Sunday School. And Mr Meikle was a good man.

When James was thirteen years old, he moved from the little school in Glen Aray to Inveraray Grammar School. But almost as soon as he enrolled he started working out ways of leaving school once and for all. His plans, however, did not always work out as he hoped they would.

'Civil engineering is a good job,' his father told him. 'That's what I'd like you to do. I know boys often leave school to work with their fathers, but being a stonemason is hard work, especially in the long winter months. In any case, you've a good brain and I think you can do better for yourself.'

That was quite a long speech for Mr Chalmers, who was a very quiet man. James listened and took heed. Being a civil engineer sounded fine to him, and better than book learning at school.

'Mr Darroch is looking for a boy to train up,' Mr Chalmers told his son not long afterwards.

'As a civil engineer?' James asked excitedly, seeing in his mind the end of school, the end of teachers and the end of homework.

'That's right,' said his father. 'But remember, you'd be starting at the very bottom as an apprentice. It takes years before you're fully trained as an engineer. After that you'd have to work your way up.'

But James didn't mind that. The thirteen-year-old lad was grinning from ear to ear.

He was not always grinning in the weeks that followed.

'There must be more to civil engineering than this,' he moaned to himself. 'The most interesting job I've done so far is carrying Mr Darroch's chain when he's out surveying. And that was only interesting because he was surveying along the shore and I could watch the fishing boats at the same time.'

It wasn't long until James knew that he didn't want to carry a chain around for the next five years. Suddenly school seemed not so bad and, after some persuading, Mr Chalmers allowed his son to abandon civil engineering and go back to the classroom.

'I'd forgotten how boring the Grammar School is,' James grumbled to his mother one day.

His father was working away from home at the time.

'There's a bark-beating job going,' the boy said. 'And you could use the extra money till Dad comes home with his pay.'

Mrs Chalmers couldn't deny that as she always seemed to be struggling to make ends meet.

'I don't know,' she said. 'Your father might not be best pleased.'

'But I'd get paid every week,' James reminded her. 'And I could always go back to school again if it didn't work out.'

His mother didn't take much persuading after that, and for the next few weeks James happily worked at bark-beating in the local woods with boys his own age and older. But when Mr Chalmers returned from working away his son was sent right back to school.

'You've too good a brain to spend your life working in the woods,' he was told. 'Study hard and get on in the world.'

'I really like working with animals,' James told his father some months later, careful to keep a business-like edge to his voice. 'And a herdsman's job could lead to better things in the future. If I worked hard at it, and I promise I would, I could end up managing a farm, maybe even owning a small herd of my own one day.'

Mr Chalmers sat silently thinking.

'And I'd get a can of milk home each day,' the fourteen-year-old went on, 'and maybe butter and cheese from time to time.'

'There could be a good future for you in that,' his father agreed, 'if you'd work at it.'

'I would,' James insisted. 'I would work hard. I'm made for working outside. Sitting in the school's not good for me.'

He caught his father's eye and dropped that argument like a hot potato!

'I'll think about it,' agreed Mr Chalmers. 'And I'll tell you when I've made up my mind.'

Knowing it was best to leave the matter alone, James did just that. But, when his father agreed to him leaving school to train as a herdsman, he could not contain himself. Punching the air with his fist, James felt as though he was punching school into the far distant past.

Two weeks later it was a very subdued teenager who took his place, yet again, in Inveraray Grammar School.

'You're back, James,' said the teacher. 'Will you be staying this time?'

A titter rumbled round the class, but stopped dead when Mr Smith looked up.

'I understand that books are more to your liking than cattle,' the teacher commented, his eyes meeting James's and holding his gaze.

'Yes, Sir,' the boy said, as his neck reddened and then his face blushed to match it.

Seeing his embarrassment, his classmates decided to come to his rescue.

'Please, Sir,' one of them said. 'I don't understand my mathematics.'

'Phew!' signed James thankfully. 'But how did Mr Smith find out that the farmer caught me reading a story book when I should have been looking after the cows! Inveraray's such a small place that everybody knows everything about everyone else. One day I'll get away from here and go where nobody knows me.'

Before he was fifteen years old James Chalmers left school for the very last time to take up a job in the office of Maclullich and Macniven, lawyers, in Inveraray. Perched on a high chair, he spent much of his time copying things he didn't really understand and didn't particularly want to. It was a bonus when he was sent out to deliver something to a nearby house or farm, and few knew better than he did the longest routes to everywhere and how best to keep out of the office.

'Hello, James,' said Mr Meikle, when he met the boy out delivering a letter.

James realised he was about to blush and just managed to prevent himself doing so by looking straight in the minister's eye.

'Hello, Mr Meikle,' he said. 'How are you?'

'It's more like me to be asking how you are, James. You've not been at Sunday School these last few weeks.'

The blush threatened again even though James still held the minister's eye.

'I'll come on Sunday,' he said. 'But I'll not be there every week because I'm a working man now.'

'So I see,' agreed Mr Meikle. 'And a fine looking one too. I look forward to seeing you on Sunday then. Goodbye, James.'

The minister shook his hand and crossed the road to speak to someone else.

'Blow! I wasn't going to go this Sunday, but I suppose I'll have to.'

James's problem was that he liked Mr Meikle very much indeed and didn't want to hurt him.

'Take this letter down to Sheriff Maclaurin,' he was told the following Tuesday.

To get to Sheriff Maclaurin's home James had to go though the Newton, which was where Mr Meikle lived. That being the case he kept his eyes open in order to avoid the minister if he should appear. After all, he'd been at Sunday School on Sunday and he didn't want to be trapped into going again!

'There he is!' the boy said to himself. 'But he's so short-sighted he can't see me yet.'

He looked around for a way of escape and quickly found one.

From then on the boy played a game with Mr Meikle that the poor minister knew nothing about. James figured out ways of dodging the short-sighted gentleman by using his own agility and speed. It worked very well nine times out of ten!

'You're getting a bad reputation, young man,' James was told by his employer soon afterwards. 'And Maclullich and Macniven don't like it.'

'No, Sir,' mumbled the boy, shifting from one foot to the other uncomfortably. 'I'm sorry, Sir.'

'It seems that if there's mischief to be done in Inveraray you're one of the young men who's making it happen.'

James, head bowed to avoid looking at his boss, suddenly noticed a spider weaving a web between the laces of the man's well-polished boots. He face broke into a smile.

'You find this amusing?' he was asked.

'No Sir,' the teenager said. 'It's not funny at all, Sir.'

'Don't let it happen again then. Get back to work.'

As he dipped his pen into his inkwell, James wondered what it was he'd promised not to let happen again. Had his boss discovered about the apples stolen from the grounds of Inveraray Castle? Or had he heard the song he'd made up about Sheriff Maclaurin? Or, horror or horrors, had he seen him down on the pier helping himself to fish without paying for them?

'It wasn't really theft,' he thought. 'Some of us were having a bonfire and we needed fish to roast on it. We were hungry.'

As James worked his way through the figures he was given to copy, he thought of Ishabel Campbell who'd spent four weeks in jail for stealing a loaf of bread.

'I bet she was hungrier than we were,' thought the boy.

A few weeks later, James Chalmers took himself back to Mr Meikle's Sunday School. 'If I don't turn up, he'll be walking the long road home to see why not,' he thought. 'In any case, I miss seeing him.'

Sunday School over, the students went back into the little church to sing, to answer questions and to hear a short talk.

'I wonder what we'll do this afternoon,' thought James, as the minister prepared to speak.

Taking a copy of a church newspaper from his jacket pocket, Mr Meikle turned the pages till he found the article for which he was looking.

'Today I'm going to read you a letter from a missionary working in Fiji.'

The letter was about cannibals who needed to hear about Jesus. It described the work being done by Christian missionaries, and finished with the need for others to go to far distant places to tell those who had never heard the name of Jesus about the Lord.

When Mr Meikle stopped speaking James's mind raced on.

'Tell us more,' he willed. 'Don't stop there.'

But the minister had read to the end of the letter. Looking over his spectacles he spoke directly to the boys in front of him.

'I wonder if there is a boy here this afternoon who will become a missionary, a boy who will one day take the Gospel to cannibals?'

It was as though the words burned through James's mind and heart. Every part of him wanted to say, 'Yes, I'll go.' But the words wouldn't come out of his mouth.

'Goodbye, James,' said Mr Meikle, as the boys left church.

'Goodbye, Sir,' answered James, hoping that the good man could read the passion in his eyes for what he had just heard.

And on his way home young, James Chalmers stopped for a moment - not to hide from a short-sighted minister - but to speak to the God of all the universe. As he pictured the cannibal tribes of the South Sea Islands James prayed, 'Make me their missionary.'

Rising to his feet James continued his walk home and then he began to wonder what Fiji was like. 'Are there hills there like the hills of Argyll?' he asked himself. 'Fiji's an island, so I suppose I'd be able to fish in the sea. Maybe I could get to know local sailors and go out with them in their boats. That would be a good way of befriending them.'

But then he remembered that these people were cannibals - they ate the bodies of people they had killed. A shiver ran up James's spine as he thought about what the word meant.

But he had told God he would be a missionary and, as far as James was concerned, there was no going back.

However, over the next fortnight James's new-found passion for mission work became a distant memory. His longing to tell the cannibals about Jesus began to melt away. There was so much to do, so many friends to see, so much to talk about. Before long Fiji was tucked safely at the back of James's mind. If he ever remembered about his promise to be a missionary, a good time with his friends was all he needed to make him forget it once again.

'Are you going to church on Sunday?' he was asked some months later.

'No, I am not. I've had enough of church,' James insisted. 'Church is for children and old people and I'm neither!'

'Well said!' laughed one of his friends. 'We thought you'd caught religion a few months ago.'

Just for a second James's conscience bothered him but he ignored it completely.

'So did I!' he laughed heartily. 'But it was like the 'flu. It hit me hard for a few days then I got better!'

Thinking that was the best joke of the night, the crowd of teenagers laughed and laughed as they headed for the woods on the hill north of Inveraray to discuss what to get up to next.

In November 1859, when James Chalmers was eighteen years old, he and his friends were crouched round a campfire making plans.

'Did you hear that two preachers from Ireland are holding meetings here in Inveraray?' one asked.

'Yes,' said another. 'We'll not be going to hear them.'

'Well...'

The boys spun round and looked at the speaker. It was Dugald.

'Are you suggesting that we should go and hear the preachers?' one demanded.

'Not exactly,' said Dugald. 'More that we should go and prevent anyone else from hearing them.'

'You mean .....?'

Dugald grinned. 'I mean the odd fit of coughing, the occasional spasm of sneezing. If we all start doing that, think about the noise!'

'And if one of us fell asleep and snored loudly,' laughed Calum, 'that would be even better.'

'Some people make a kind of grunting sound when they are snoring,' Dugald laughed, giving a demonstration at the same time. Very shortly all the boys were trying it out - snorting and sneezing and snoring their heads off.

'I like it!' Dugald said. 'Where are the meetings being held?'

'The one tomorrow is in the joiner's loft in the Maltland.'

'We'll show them how religious the young men of Inveraray are. Let's all turn up at the meeting!'

In the joiner's loft

'Hello, Archie,' James said, as he entered Archibald MacNicoll's shop early the following evening. 'How are you today?'

'I'm fine, James. What about yourself?'

The two friends sat down side by side and sorted out the world as good friends do. Not a word did James say about the mischief his friends were planning because he knew Archie wouldn't approve.

'Are you going to the meeting in the joiner's loft?' Archie MacNicoll asked.

James couldn't think if he should say yes or no. His friends were going to cause trouble. James was planning that too. Before he could reply Archie continued, 'I think you should go. God might speak to you there.'

'If God wants to speak to me, he knows where to find me any day of the week,' scoffed James. 'He doesn't have to speak through an Irish preacher.'

'I think you're running away from God,' his friend said sadly.

'Well if God is God he'll be able to run faster than I can, so I suppose he'll catch up with me sooner or later.'

Every suggestion Archie MacNicol made was countered by a mocking comment from his friend.

'Look,' said the shopkeeper eventually, 'here's a Bible. It's not long till the meeting's due to start. Just go, will you?'

James looked out at the rain beating down and couldn't

think of one single excuse. Argyllshire rain comes down in sheets in November and suddenly the joiner's loft seemed a better place to be than the long road home.

'OK, I'll go just this once. But once will be enough. Don't pester me to go another night.'

James left the shop, pulled his coat over his head and ran through the rain to the Maltland. Turning off the street at the bottom of the stairs to the joiner's loft, he took his coat from his head and realised that the meeting had started. The sound of singing came down the stairs to meet him.

'That's lovely,' he thought, much to his great surprise.

Climbing quietly up the steps in order not to disturb the meeting, he opened the door and went in.

'What a crowd!' James said to himself, as he tried to find a seat.

That night the Irish speaker preached his heart out on the subject of God calling people to come to him. As he listened in the absolute silence of the meeting to the talk, James realised that the rain had kept his friends away. There were no piercing whistles, no fits of coughing or spasms of sneezing and no sleepy young people snoring their way loudly through the meeting. It felt as though there was just God and James Chalmers in the joiner's loft, and that God was speaking.

'Here's your Bible,' James said, handing the book into his friend's house on his way home after the meeting.

'What did you think of the speaker?' Archie asked.

James had nothing to say. The thought of what he had very nearly done to disrupt the meeting made him want to sit down and weep.

'Goodnight,' was all he managed.

'Goodnight,' Archie called after him. 'And God bless you.'

'Are you up to some fun and games?' Dugald asked, when he met James in the street the next day. 'This looks like a better night for it. The rain last night was enough to wash Inveraray away!'

'No, thanks,' replied James. 'Count me out.'

'Ohhhh. Why would that be?'

'Just count me out,' the young man said firmly. 'Count me out tonight and every night the meetings are on.'

'So you've caught religious 'flu again, have you?' teased Dugald unkindly. 'Did it start with a fit of sneezing then?'

James looked at his friend sadly and walked away.

The following Sunday evening Dugald and his cronies saw James going in the door of the church.

'James has still got a good dose of religious flu,' laughed Dugald. 'But another day or two should see him improving.'

If only Dugald had known the truth of what he said. James was sickening, but it was with sin-sickness. For the first time he had realised what a sinner he was and just how offensive his sins were to God. When he left the church that night James thought he was lost forever, that he was going straight to hell and nothing could stop him. But the following night did see an improvement. The good and patient Mr Meikle explained to James Chalmers that Jesus had died to take away his sins.

'Does that mean I can be saved?' the teenager asked, hardly daring to believe that could be true.

'Yes, it certainly does,' said Mr Meikle. 'The blood

Jesus shed on the cross washes away the sins of those who trust in the Lord as Saviour.'

'All of them?' asked James, amazed at the possibility.

'All of them,' stated the minister firmly. 'All in the past and all in the future, every last one of them.'

It seemed too good to be true, too wonderful to be possible, too amazing for words.

James Chalmers, born in August 1841, was born again eighteen years later, in November 1859!

The January storms blew fierce that year and a boat was overdue. A worried group of people stood at the pier and watched for any sign of it. Dugald was among them, as was James.

'You should be on your knees praying for the crew,' Dugald hissed. 'If God's in heaven you should be begging him to save them!'

James drew back and leant against the gas lamp stand. The light had been out for hours because of the wind. Praying with every ounce of his strength the young man was totally oblivious to what was going on around him. He didn't hear the shout half-an-hour later when the boat was sighted, nor did he see the ropes thrown against the wind and grabbed by willing hands on shore. He was concentrating so much on pouring out his prayers for the sailors whose lives were in danger that he didn't hear the laughter and tears of relief as the men, all of them, were pulled to land, to safety. The first James knew was when Dugald hit him hard on the shoulder.

'You can stop praying now,' he shouted above the storm. 'It worked.'

Turning his back on an exhausted James, Dugald pushed

his hands deep in his coat pockets and strode off into the night.

As James walked home he faced up to a memory that had troubled him every day since he became a Christian.

'Years ago I promised God that I'd be a missionary. What am I going to do about it?'

The woods through which he was walking provided no answer.

'I can't go to college to train to be a missionary because I don't have the money to pay for it. And I can't go overseas without training.'

He strode on, turning the matter over and over in his mind.

'I suppose I could start by being a missionary here in Scotland,' he thought. 'There are plenty of people here who don't believe in Jesus. There's Dugald for a start. And Calum. Maybe this is where I'm meant to be a missionary.'

There was a lull in the storm as he walked up the hill towards home and it wasn't long before he could see the light in the living-room window.

'Are they safe?' Mrs Chalmers asked, as soon as James opened the door.

'They're safe home,' he said. 'All of them.'

'Thank the Lord for that,' his mother breathed. 'I couldn't bear the thought of more families losing their menfolk. That's the worst of living beside the sea.'

That night James's dreams came in a confusing mix. There were fishing boats battling to reach Inveraray and ships sailing to faraway places with missionaries on board.

He saw himself preaching in a mud hut in a foreign land and in a cottage that he vaguely recognised. All he knew in the morning was that he was shattered and desperately needed a long lie-in.

'You'll be late for work,' his mother warned him.

'No I won't,' he said. 'I'll take the road quickly and be there on time.'

'There's a letter for Sheriff Maclaurin,' he was told soon after arriving in the office.

By then he was working for another firm in Inveraray, in the office of Wilson and Douglas, but he still went on regular errands to the Sheriff.

'Yes, Sir,' said James, putting his coat back on.

As he walked along the road he smiled to himself. 'I used to watch for Mr Meikle and get out of his way before he saw me, now I'm watching for him because I want his advice!'

Knowing the letter was urgent, James took it straight to Sheriff Maclaurin. But he walked the long way back and, sure enough, met the minister.

'I'll walk you to the office, James, and we can talk along the way. Now, what is it you want to discuss?'

James told Mr Meikle what was in his mind and waited for his reply. The minister walked a little way in silence then spoke his mind.

'What you've told me is no surprise, my boy, for I know you through and through. You're right in thinking that you should be a missionary right here in Argyll, but that doesn't mean that God doesn't want you overseas eventually.'

'But the cost of the training ... I don't earn that kind of money. And my parents hardly have enough to keep themselves and my sisters.'

'I know that, but there are ways and means.'

'What do you mean, Mr Meikle?'

'Many students work while they're studying and manage to earn enough to keep themselves, you know.'

'But even if I could do that, I didn't work hard enough at school to get into college in the first place.'

Mr Meikle chuckled.

'What are you laughing at?' James asked, puzzled at this break in their serious discussion.

'I'm laughing at the memory of your Grammar School education, and the effort to which you went to avoid it! Remember? You left school to work with a civil engineer. Then you left to work as a woodsman. Not content with that, you left to take a job as a stockman! No wonder you're not well prepared for college!'

Much to his surprise James found himself laughing too.

'Thanks, Mr Meikle,' he said, when they reached the door of Wilson and Douglas.

'We'll talk again,' the minister assured him. 'And we can both do some thinking before that.'

The next time James 'accidentally' bumped into Mr Meikle they got right into the subject of missionary training immediately.

'I'm happy to work my way through college,' James said, 'if they'll only accept me as a student.'

'And I'm happy to give you lessons to get you up to college standard,' added Mr Meikle.

James stopped in his tracks and swung round to face the minister.

'You'd do that?'

Mr Meikle smiled kindly.

'I'd happily do that. You and I are in this together, young James Chalmers.'

'You've no time for your old friends now,' Dugald complained, when he met James in the street. 'You're either at the minister's or you're taking meetings in one house or another. We used to have good times together, you and me. It doesn't feel good just to be dumped.'

James looked at his old schoolmate.

'I didn't mean to dump you,' he said. 'I just thought you'd not want to know me now I'm a Christian.'

'Did it never occur to you that I might be interested in knowing what you believe?'

'No,' admitted James. 'It didn't, and I'm really sorry.'

'Meet you tonight?'

'I'm sorry, I'm speaking at a meeting at Furnace tonight. But if you want to come with me, we could talk on the way ...'

'OK,' agreed Dugald, 'That's what I'll do. But don't be surprised if I argue with what you've said on the way back.'

James slapped his friend on the back. 'I'd enjoy that,' he laughed. 'You'll keep me in my place.'

That was the first of many discussions Dugald and James had. And, when Dugald went off to sea a few months later, James knew that even if his friend was not a Christian, he was certainly very interested.

'There's someone coming to Inveraray I think you'd like to meet,' said Mr Meikle, in a break from their Latin lesson. 'He's an Ayrshire man called William Turner. His brother, Dr George Turner, is a missionary in Samoa, in the South Sea Islands.'

'When's he coming?' James asked excitedly.

'This summer,' said the minister. 'He's very interested in what's happening in this part of Scotland.'

'I can't wait to meet him! Do you think he'll know much about missionary work?'

Mr Meikle laughed. 'I know he does!'

So when in the summer of 1860 James met William Turner their conversation was mostly about mission work. By the time Mr Turner left for home James knew in his heart that the call he had answered when he was just a boy was a real call from God. The Lord did want him to be a missionary overseas, amazing and almost impossible as it seemed. In the year that followed even Mr Meikle was surprised at the amount of work his young student did in preparation.

It was in 1861 that James packed up his few belongings and set off for Glasgow, sixty-five miles away.

'Imagine you being a missionary,' said his young sister. 'I'll not know how to talk to you when you come home again.'

'I'm only going to be a Glasgow City Missionary,' laughed James. 'I'll not come back talking a foreign language!'

'But you're still hoping to go overseas after that, aren't you?' she asked.

'Yes,' he admitted. 'But it could take years to get all the training I'll need.'

'Your area is the High Street,' James was told at the Glasgow City Mission Headquarters. 'You've a mission hall to look after and the meetings there are your responsibility. You'll not find it an easy job for that's a sinful dark area.

We'll be praying for you.'

'Thank you, Sir,' said James.

When he arrived at the mission hall there was someone there before him.

'Who're you?' said the man who was leaning against the door.

'I'm the new missionary. My name's James Chalmers.'

'You'll be a highlander from your accent,' announced the man. 'And you'll have some money on you for a poor soul like me.'

James had to stand back from his companion because the smell of drink was so strong.

'If you come in I'll make you a cup of tea instead.'

The man spat in James's face.

'If tea's all you're offering you're no good to me!'

Turning his back, he strode angrily away. As James wiped his face he remembered reading in the Bible that before he was crucified men spat on Jesus.

Having unpacked his things, the new missionary set about examining the hall. That done, James decided to walk round the High Street to see what he could see.

'Are you the new missionary?' a tiny woman asked.

'Yes,' he said. 'I'm James Chalmers.'

'Well, Mr Chalmers, I'm so pleased you're here. Can you help me?'

'Tell me what the trouble is,' he said kindly, 'and I'll see if I can.'

'It's my daughter,' explained the woman. 'She's been sick for days and we've no money for a doctor. Can you come and pray for her? That'll maybe help.'

James followed the poor woman up an alleyway and

into a dark hovel of a home. It took a minute for him to focus on the young girl who lay on a bundle of rags on the floor. The smell that hit him nearly made him sick. Reaching out, he took the girl by the hand.

'I'm James Chalmers, the new missionary,' he said. 'Would you like me to pray for you?'

The poor girl nodded and closed her eyes while he prayed. Her breathing was rasping and sore, and her mother brought some water in a bowl for her to drink.

'Has she eaten today?' James asked.

The woman burst into tears. 'We've no food. My man's away looking for work and we've no food till he finds a job ... or steals something for us to eat.'

James rose from the floor. 'I'll be back,' he said. 'I'll not be long.'

Rushing round the corner to the mission hall, he found his bag of oatmeal and made some thin porridge that he carried the short distance to the first home in Glasgow that was open to his help.

'Here,' he said, squatting down on the floor beside the sick girl. 'Drink some of this. Just take a little mouthful at a time.'

'And this is for you,' he added, handing a cloth bag to the woman at his side. 'It's oatmeal. Make yourself some porridge or you'll not have the strength to nurse your daughter.'

'God bless you, Mr Chalmers,' the woman said through tears of sheer relief.

'I'll call back tomorrow,' said James. 'And I'll try to bring some clean water for you to give her to drink.'

On his way back round to the mission hall the young man met two orphan boys, aged about eleven and ten, though they were far too small for their ages.

'Are you goin' to have a meetin' we can come to?' one of them asked.

'Yes, I am,' said James, looking at the two scraps whose eager and filthy faces looked up at his.

'Will there be tea at the meetin'?' asked the smaller of the two.

James glanced down to the boy's stick-like arms and legs, to his ragged clothes and his filthy bare feet.

'Yes,' he said, smiling. 'There'll be tea at the meetings. And you can have two cups if you like. By the way, what are your names? I'm Mr Chalmers.'

'I'm Charlie,' said the older boy. 'And m' mate's Tom. We don't 'ave other names, so when we grow up we'll just 'ave to be Mr Charlie and Mr Tom.'

Back in the quietness of his mission hall James thought about his first day in Glasgow. He knew there were respectable people in the High Street area, but there were others, like those he'd already met, who were as pathetic as could be.

'There's so much work to be done here,' he thought. 'How am I ever going to do it?'

Door knocking

'I wonder who that is at the door,' said William Turner. 'It's not the usual time of day for visitors.'

The maid knocked on the sitting room door, opened it, and announced, 'There's a Mr James Chalmers here to see you, Sir.'

'Show him in!' laughed William. 'I knew he was due in Glasgow this week and hoped he'd come to see us soon.'

James entered the room hesitantly. It wasn't a very grand house, but it was much more impressive than any he'd been in before. Even Mr Meikle's home in Inveraray wasn't anything like a house in Glasgow.

'Good to see you, my lad,' William said. 'And this is my brother Dr George Turner. I've told you about him.'

'And he's told me about you,' smiled George. 'You're the young man from Argyll who has come to work for Glasgow City Mission. It's good to meet you.'

'Bring us tea, please,' William told the maid, who closed the door quietly behind her.

'Well, James, what do you think of the great city of Glasgow?' asked William.

'It's a fearful place,' the young missionary said. 'I thought I'd seen poverty at home in Inveraray, but it's nothing to the poverty around the High Street. At least in the country people could grow fresh vegetables. And even if they'd no well near their house, they could get clean water from a nearby stream. The first day I was here I saw a poor sick girl drinking water that I'd not have given to sheep!'

'The terrible thing is that some of the worst diseases are carried in dirty water,' commented Dr George. 'People weakened by illness who drink the stuff are likely to catch something even worse than they already have.'

'I suppose I'll get used to seeing such things,' James thought aloud.

William looked up sharply. 'I sincerely hope you will not! The day you become used to seeing such sights is the day you'll lose the desire to change things. My advice to you is this, wherever you go in the world keep Inveraray in your mind. Never lose sight of the fact that poor people can be fed, clean water can he found, and that people on their own need not be lonely.'

'That's good advice,' said Dr George. 'I've travelled to the furthest parts of the world and found it to be true.'

When the maid came back into the room with tea things on a tray William went to help her hand the cups out.

'Now, young man,' said Dr George, 'I hear that you think the Lord is calling you to serve him as a missionary overseas.'

'Yes, Sir,' James agreed. 'Even as a boy, before I became a Christian, that's what I thought. Mind you, I put it to the back of my mind for years. But since I trusted in the Lord Jesus the thought just won't go away.'

'So why have you come to work in Glasgow?'

'Mr Meikle, my minister back home, said it would be good experience and that it would allow me to save a little money towards paying for my training while being an active missionary at the same time.'

'A wise man, Mr Meikle,' commented William, as he handed his brother a cup of tea. 'What training do you mean to take?' asked George.

'I think I should train to be a minister. That would be the best thing to do before going overseas. But tell me about your work Dr Turner,' asked James.

Dr George Turner looked lost in thought. Stretching his legs out, he drank half of his cup of tea before beginning his answer.

'I went out to Samoa in 1841,' he began.

'That was the year I was born,' James thought.

'Basically my work has been in setting up a training school for preachers at Malua. That may sound rather tame, but I've had my adventures all right.'

'Have you ever met cannibals?' asked James.

'Yes, I have. And I can tell you there have been times when I've feared for my life.'

'Like on the island of Tanna,' suggested William.

'Some terrible things happened on Tanna right enough,' his brother agreed. 'But, James, I've known cannibals who became Christians, and that's a most wonderful thing to see!'

The talk could have gone on all afternoon, but the Glasgow City missionary had work to do.

'Hello you two!' laughed James. 'You've come to the meeting after all.'

'Course we did!' said Tom.

'Did you think we'd not come for our two cups of tea?' asked Charlie.

By the time the meeting was due to begin the mission hall was nearly full of children. One or two were well enough dressed and reasonably clean, but most looked as though it was some time since they'd had any serious encounter with soap and water.

'What's that running about, Sir?' asked one boy, when the meeting had just begun. He pointed to the corner of the room behind where James was standing.

When the city missionary turned round to look, several small pebbles hit him on the back and a larger one thumped him on the head. He spun round.

'Who threw these?' he demanded.

The children, over 80 of them, looked as though he was speaking in a foreign language. Their faces read, 'Does he think any of US would do a thing like that?'

James decided that singing would keep them busy so he told them which hymn they would sing. Most sang in tune, but somewhere in the hall a boy's voice shouted 'boom, boom, boom.' As soon as James worked out which part of the hall it was coming from it changed to somewhere else. From the back to the front the boom bounced, with never a break between beats. By the third verse of the hymn most of those who had begun singing well enough had given up, and by the end of the fourth verse James was singing alone. Every child in the hall was chanting 'boom, boom, boom!'

The prayer that followed was relatively quietly received until the Amen, when James nearly jumped out of his skin as it seemed that every single child screamed the word at the top of his or her voice!

'What am I going to do with them?' he wondered. 'They've just come to make a fool of me ... and they're succeeding!'

'Right, you lot,' the new missionary said at the top of

his voice. It was the only way he could be heard. 'I'm going to tell you a true story, but I'm not going to shout a single word of it. If you want to hear me, be quiet and listen. If you're not quiet enough, I'll just stop speaking and you'll never hear the end of the story.'

'A few years ago, when I was not much older than some of you,' he began quietly, 'I was every bit as mischievous as you all are.'

There was a ripple of chatter though most seemed to be listening.

'Shoosh!' said someone near the front. 'We want to hear what he's got to say for himself.'

James began another sentence, but several boys talking loudly drowned it out.

'Shoosh, or we'll come and shoosh you!' Charlie shouted.

'And I'll come and shoosh you too!' added Tom, all ten years of him.

Amazingly the hall fell silent and James began his story again.

'Two Irishmen came to the town I lived in to hold Christian meetings. My friends and I decided we'd go along. But rather than listen to what they were saying we'd make as much noise as we could so that nobody would be able to hear the speakers.'

James stopped for a minute to decide how best to tell what happened next. There wasn't a sound in the whole mission hall.

'One of my friends, I think it might have been Dugald, suggested that we sit at the back and all pretend to have a fierce fit of coughing. Then someone else said that sneezing could be good fun too. It was almost as though we were

45

organising a massive attack of hay fever even though it was
the month of November!'

Still not a single sound disturbed what James was
saying.

'We were getting really excited by then. One of the lads
came up with a great idea. He said that after we'd coughed
ourselves hoarse and sneezed fit to burst we could pretend
we were so bored that we'd fallen asleep ... and snore for
all we were worth!'

James then began to grunt and whistle through his nose
just like Dugald and Calum had done all those years ago.
It went down a treat! The place erupted with laughter that
faded into total silence to let the city missionary speak.

'Well,' said James. 'The night of the meeting came and
it poured with rain. I went into a friend's shop to shelter
and he persuaded me to go to the meeting to listen to what
was being said. He even gave me a Bible to take. Now, the
rain was so awful that my friends didn't turn up and I found
myself there on my own, actually listening to what the
Irishmen were saying! And do you know what happened?'

Not a sound came from his audience.

'That night it was as though God spoke right to me, as
though I was the only person in the whole room apart from
the speakers.'

'What did he say?' asked Charlie.

'God said that he was calling me to follow him, calling
me to believe in Jesus.'

Charlie's eyes were wide open. 'Did you?'

'Not that night,' admitted James. 'But a couple of days
later I asked Jesus to forgive all my sins. And he did. That
was the day I became a Christian.'

'You really were a sinner,' Tom called out quietly. 'You

were going to do an awful thing at the meeting, weren't you?'

'Yes,' James agreed. 'But God stopped me in my tracks and made me listen to what he had to say from the Bible.'

The young city missionary looked round the silent hall.

'Would you like me to tell you something from the Bible?'

Heads nodded everywhere.

James stood in front of some of the dirtiest and smelliest children in the whole of Scotland and told them that Jesus wanted children like them to come to him, to trust in him, to have faith in him.

'Does Jesus really want folk like us,' asked Charlie, wiping his nose on his sleeve.

'He really does,' James told him. 'He really truly does.'

For the eight months that followed, James Chalmers worked hard as a Glasgow City Missionary.

'What're you doin'?' Charlie asked most mornings. He and Tom seemed to spend their time outside or inside the mission hall.

'I'm going visiting?'

'Who're you visiting?'

'I don't know yet. I'm just going to knock at each door I come to along the street and speak to whoever answers it.'

'What'll you speak to them about?'

'Don't be stupid,' interrupted Tom. 'He's only got one subject. He's always trying to speak about Jesus.'

'S'pose so,' Charlie agreed. 'See you later!'

'What're you doin'?' asked Charlie the next morning.

'I'm going to help an old man clean the room he lives in?'

'Why?'

'Because it's so dirty it's making him sick.'

'Why're you doin' it?'

'I'm doing it because Jesus wants me to help.'

'You're daft!'

James still hadn't reached the lane that led up to the old man's house when the sound of bare feet running made him turn round.

'We've come to help you,' said Charlie and Tom together. 'But don't you dare tell anyone!'

The same question met James when he left home the following day.

'What're you doin'?'

'There's a poor sick girl needing visited,' he explained. 'She's doesn't have very long to live and she's asked me to go and see her.'

'You're on your own on that one,' Tom said. 'If you see a dead person you're near dead yourself.'

James didn't take time to discuss the boy's comment; he was in too much of a hurry to tell the girl about the Lord Jesus Christ before she died.

In the course of his work as a city missionary James knocked on door after door, going round his district street after street, day after day. Some of his friends back home in Inveraray would have thought he was doing the most boring job in the world. James did not. Behind every door was a different person, every single one of whom needed to know about Jesus.

'I never get tired of talking about the Lord,' James wrote home to a friend. 'But I think some people get tired of listening to me!'

There was one door in Glasgow that James knocked on as often as he possibly could. It was William Hunter's door, and he didn't just enjoy going there because everything in that home was clean and fresh and nothing smelled of sick or urine or stale perspiration … or just old dirt. James especially enjoyed going there because Dr George was spending some months with his brother, and the doctor and city missionary never ran out of things to talk about.

'I won't be going abroad again until my work here is finished,' Dr George explained.

'Tell me more about what you are doing here?' asked James.

Dr George reached for some papers nearby and handed them to his visitor. 'Try reading this,' he suggested.

The young man looked at the sheet of strange words. 'I can't,' he laughed. 'I've no idea what it says.'

'Maybe you will one day,' smiled the doctor. 'The Bible has been translated into the Samoan language and I'm here to oversee its printing. When I go back the Bible in Samoan will go with me. Can you just imagine the welcome I'll be given by the Christians there when I return?'

'Is your heart set on being a Glasgow City Missionary now?' Dr George asked, when James called one day. 'Or do you still think God is calling you overseas?'

'I believe he is,' the young man said. 'I love my work here, but it feels as though I'm just here for a while, that God has other things he wants me to do.'

'Well, then,' said the doctor, 'I've a suggestion. I don't think you should train for anything before applying to be a missionary. I think you should apply to the London Missionary Society right away. If they accept you, they'll train you in the work they think you should be doing.'

'But ....'

'No buts,' insisted Dr George, 'just go away and think and pray about it.'

That was how James Chalmers came to be accepted as a trainee missionary, and why he moved to Cheshunt College in London eight months after leaving Inveraray.

'How on earth will I cope in England?' he asked himself anxiously.

It was as though he thought England was on the other side of the world.

The good ship John Williams

'Where do you come from?' someone asked James on their first day at Cheshunt.

'I'm from Inveraray on the west coast of Scotland,' he replied.

'And you?'

'I'm from Birmingham, which is almost as far from any coast of England as you can be.'

'Poor soul,' commented James. 'There's no part of Scotland more than about 40 miles from the sea. And that's how it should be. Living beside the sea does us good, because it reminds us how small we are.'

'Cheshunt is full of English people,' James exclaimed one morning. 'There's hardly a Scot in the place.'

One of his fellow students burst out laughing. 'Do you mean to tell me that you are surprised that England is mostly populated by the English?'

The Scot grinned. 'I suppose it is a bit daft,' he admitted. 'But it just hadn't occurred to me.'

Dr Reynolds, Principal of Cheshunt College, was passing at the time.

'If you ever go to France, Mr Chalmers, you'll discover that it's mostly French people who live there.'

The old principal walked off chortling at his own joke.

Being a college student was a completely new experience for James, but he took to it like a duck to water and loved it. He studied hard … and he played hard too.

'What's that?' yelled a student one night, when he and his friends met for a chat before bed.

Everyone's eyes turned towards the door, and several of the men screamed when they saw a brown bear entering on all fours! It padded across the room to the petrified students and grabbed one of them in a powerful hug.

'Pop' the gas light went out. In the darkness the bear released its hold on the gibbering student and rubbed against one or two of the others. Screams sliced through the darkness. When the light went back on again there was James dressed in a bearskin!

'Where did you get that?' demanded his astonished friends.

'Mr Tugwell, who used to be a missionary in North America, brought the skin back home with him. I was thinking that I could do with a souvenir like this to take back with me to Scotland. Maybe I'll take an Englishman!'

His classmates laughed at the thought of one of them being squashed into James Chalmers' luggage.

James was not one of those people who can play tricks on others but not accept it when others play tricks on them.

'Let's catch him out,' a fellow student said to a group of others not long after the bear incident. 'I've a plan.'

Full of interest the others waited to hear what it was.

'Let's lock him in his room then stuff his keyhole with cayenne pepper.'

'Eh?' gasped his friend. 'Why?'

'Well,' the instigator explained, 'we can set light to the pepper from the outside of the door and the fumes will fill his room till he can't stand it any more.'

'I take it we let him out then,' someone suggested.

'No, when he can't open the door he'll rush to the window, open it wide and stick his head out for fresh air.'

'So what?' asked one of the young men.

'So you'll be on the roof above his window with a bucket of water ready to pour it over him!'

Having been thoroughly taken in by the bear the students agreed to carry out the plan. Everything went exactly as arranged and James Chalmers, sneezing and soaked, thought it was the greatest of good fun!

'I'm looking for a preacher for Hertford Heath,' Principal Reynolds said. 'Do I have any volunteers?'

'Would you like me to go?' James offered.

'It's a sixteen-mile round trip,' whispered his friend who was sitting right behind him.

'I'm used to long walks and long rides,' the Scot told his friend afterwards. 'It's a long way from Inveraray to anywhere. Distance doesn't bother me.'

'Maybe God will send you to the other side of the world to work if you're as willing a traveller as all that!'

James became a favourite preacher at Hertford Heath and was asked to go there quite regularly.

'Are you coming boating on the River Lea,' someone asked James on a fine afternoon.

'I don't think so,' he said. 'I'm not feeling very well. Maybe I'll bring a book down to the river later.'

When he did arrive at the Lea he discovered some of his fellow students boating and others playing about in the deep water. He settled down in the shade to read his book.

'They're having a great time,' he thought, looking up a short while later. Then something caught his eye. One of the students was out of his depth and another was swimming out to help him. James jumped to his feet. The rescuer was being dragged under!

'Swim out and make a chain of hands!' he yelled to the crowd that didn't realise their friends were in danger.

Hearing the urgency in his voice, and seeing James rushing into the water, they did exactly as they were told. With strong strokes the young Scot was soon beside the two who were on the point of going under for the very last time. Grabbing one with each hand he turned on to his back and kicked the water with slow powerful beats that took them in the direction of the shore. Just as his strength began to fail he reached the first hand in the chain. Using the men in the chain as an anchor and guide he moved his burdens painfully slowly towards safety until he was within his depth. Then he half swam, half staggered, to the shore leaving the others to deal with the two coughing and spluttering young men.

'James Chalmers has made quite an impression during his time here,' said Dr Reynolds, towards the end of his studies. 'He's worked hard, though he's not a brilliant student, but he'll be remembered for other things too.'

'Not least saving two of his fellow students from drowning,' said his colleague.

'Yes, there's that, of course,' Dr Reynolds agreed. 'But I

was really thinking more of his personality. He's serious when he needs to be and terrific fun when the opportunity allows it. But do you know what I'll remember most about him?'

'What's that?'

'I'll remember his prayers. When James Chalmers prays he sounds like a little child talking to his father.'

'I know exactly what you mean,' the other man agreed. 'He's a real man of prayer.'

'What are you going to do when you finish at Cheshunt?' a member of the church at Hertford Heath asked James on his last Sunday there.

'For the next year I'm going to stay at Farquhar House in Highgate and study under Dr John Wardlaw there.'

'Is that run by the London Missionary Society?'

'Yes, they opened it just three years ago, in 1861, to train their own missionaries.'

'What will you be studying?'

'A mixture of subjects including some basic medicine, practical skills that will be useful when I'm a missionary, and I hope to make a start on the Rarotongan language.'

'I didn't know that the Mission was sending you to Rarotonga,' the man said, very interested in the news.

'Neither did I until recently,' laughed James. 'It's a strange thing, for many years ago, when I was a young teenager at home in Inveraray, my minister told us about the South Sea Islands and I felt I should go there. Now it seems, after all these years, that I will be going to the South Seas after all!'

From Highgate James moved with his friend, Saville, to Woolwich where he continued his study of Rarotongan.

'It's a happy coincidence that we're going to live with Mr and Mrs Hercus,' commented Saville. 'Especially as you seem to be so fond of his niece, Jeanie. I think you should tell me more about that young woman.'

'Now,' laughed James, 'that's a subject I'm happy to talk about. Where will I begin?'

'The beginning?' suggested Saville.

'What a good idea!' James said, 'though the beginning of her story is rather sad. Jeanie is the eldest of four children and their mother died when she was just five years old. I suppose that's partly why she's such a practical and helpful person.'

'I see what you mean about a sad start to her story. I hope things got better for her after that.'

'Judge for yourself,' suggested James. 'When she was fourteen her grandfather died. He had been a minister in Kirkwall, in the Orkney Islands. Jeanie moved to Orkney and looked after her grandmother until she died five years later. She then returned to her home in Greenock near Glasgow.'

'And Glasgow was where you met her?'

'That's right. Her family moved there about the same time as I went to work as a Glasgow City Missionary. From Glasgow Jeanie moved to Leeds, where she works as a schoolteacher.'

'Jeanie Hercus sounds as though she would make a splendid missionary's wife,' commented Saville.

'I've been thinking that myself,' James said, grinning from ear to ear.

The London Missionary Society made their plans and told the missionary-to-be what work he was going to do.

'It has been decided that I'll go to one of the islands in the Hervey Group to start with. I'll have the charge of a church with over 500 members and a school of about 700 children,' he wrote in a letter on 17th March, 1865. 'The island has a population of 3,000. But I don't expect to remain there long as I hope to have more direct missionary work. There are still very many islands in the South Seas where Christ is totally unknown.'

The desire to be on his way to the South Seas burned strong in James's heart but the sad matter of a ship being lost held him back, as he went on to write in the same letter. 'Our last missionary ship was lost. They have now begun building one in Aberdeen which cannot be ready before the end of the year. So we shall have to be in this country till then.'

That summer was a long one for James, but eventually a date was set for his wedding to Jeanie Hercus and for his ordination as a minister. These two big events in his life were just two days apart. He and Jeanie were married in Greenock on 17th October and his ordination to the ministry was on 19th October 1865.

'I thought we'd be away in 1865,' James said, on the last day of the year.

'It's only four more days now,' his wife laughed.

'I can't wait!' grinned James. 'It's like having a wonderful dream and waking up to discover it wasn't a dream after all!'

January 4th dawned. The young couple, along with several other missionaries, said goodbye to their homeland and to those who had come to see them off.

'Weigh anchor!' yelled Captain Williams.

'Weigh anchor!' the ship's Mate, repeated.

With clanking and rattling, with scraping and scratching, the anchor was hauled up from the sea bed and the good ship *John Williams* eased from the quay at Gravesend, turned to catch the wind in her sails and headed out to sea.

'This is the first day of our great adventure,' Jeanie said, finding her sea legs. 'I wonder what the future holds for us.'

As the *John Williams* sailed out into the English Channel a gale blew up that sent some of the passengers to their cabins to lie down and others to their knees to pray.

'This is a fierce storm, right enough,' said the Mate, grabbing the rail of the ship to save himself from being blown across the deck.

James, who had loved the sea since boyhood, let a wave lash over him.

'What're you doing, man?' the Mate asked. 'Get below deck out of the teeth of the gale!'

'I'm happiest in the thick of it,' James yelled over the storm. 'And if you need extra hands, you can have mine.'

The following day the storm had become even more violent.

'Get as many men as possible to come and help us!' shouted Captain Williams, who had heard from the Mate that James was a natural seaman and that several of the other missionaries were as well.

'Haul that rope in!' some were told, and they struggled to do so for it seemed to weigh a ton with the water it held.

'Help bring down that sail before it's ripped to shreds,'

others were ordered, and they gripped the ropes to lower the sail with such effort that the skin was taken off the palms of their hands.

'Are we going to sink?' one of the women asked Jeanie.

'I doubt it,' James's wife said. 'If God wants us to work for him in the South Seas he won't have us all drowned in the English Channel.'

Suddenly a wave hit the *John Williams* with such violence that she listed far over to port. Jeanie and her companion were thrown to the floor. A second wave hit the ship on its starboard side and they found themselves sliding among all their possessions to the other side of the cabin.

'Man the pumps!' ordered the Captain. 'We're taking in water!'

James and one of the sailors took a pump between them and through the hours of darkness they bent their backs over it, soaked with sweat and sea water and more sea water as wave after wave hit the boat.

'Take a rest and relieve us in an hour,' the two were told, when they had all but collapsed.

James went below deck and found his wife on her knees praying.

'Are we sinking?' she asked, when she heard him coming.

'No, but we're being bounced around like a cork. I'm more worried about the new timbers being damaged than about us sinking.'

'Do you think we'll drown?' Jeanie asked.

'If God wants us to work for him in the South Seas he won't have us all drowned in the English Channel,' her soaked and exhausted husband told her.

When James heard his wife laughing he struggled to open his eyes. Was she delirious?

'That's exactly what I said a few hours ago!' she explained. 'But I suppose it's also true that if God wants to take us home to heaven today he might do it by letting the ship go down in the storm.'

'So he might,' agreed James, who was almost asleep. 'And heaven would be twice wonderful after this!'

Jeanie tried to change her husband's wet clothes as he slept, then wrapped him in a blanket and prayed.

'Mr Chalmers!' a voice yelled from the cabin door. 'You're needed to relieve at the pumps!'

James was immediately awake and on his feet.

'God bless you!' Jeanie called after him.

And as she tried to settle down to pray a tremendous wave hit the port side of the ship. Things seemed to fall from everywhere. Jeanie staggered to avoid them and then landed in a heap on the floor of her cabin. Suddenly a crash rang throughout the ship and the *John Williams* shuddered as though taking her very last breath. A wet trickle ran down Jeanie's back. Was it blood? Had something cut her badly? Was it water? Had the sea won the battle?

Shipwrecked!

When the storm eventually blew itself out the Captain and Mate decided that the *John Williams* had taken such a battering that they should return to Weymouth for repairs. It took more than two weeks to make the ship seaworthy. After setting off for a second time, it seems that the voyage was less eventful.

'April 25 1866,' wrote James, at the top of a sheet of paper. 'We're now within 900 miles of Adelaide in Australia and hope to get there soon. It has been a truly happy, pleasant and blessed time for us all. We have felt none of the boredom of sea life as there has been so much of interest to see and do. I've taken a Bible class and prayer meeting with the men on board and some of them have become Christians.'

James, who was sitting on deck writing, looked out at the calm blue sea all around him and remembered back to more stormy days.

'After leaving Weymouth we had a slight touch of seasickness … I hope we won't now become like the sailors and be land-sick when we reach shore after being such a long time at sea. My wife has proved to be the best sailor of all the ladies. In fact, she's been better than some of the men!'

Three weeks later, on 20ᵗʰ May, the ship docked at Adelaide. Jeanie's father, who had gone to live in New

Zealand, had travelled to Australia to welcome them. The next few weeks were spent travelling around Australia getting to know some of the Christians there. In August they climbed aboard the *John Williams* in Sydney harbour and set off once again, this time for the South Sea Islands, only to return three weeks later with the ship badly damaged and in need of serious repair. It was October before they left Australia on what they hoped would be the last lap of their long journey.

'Show me on the map exactly where we're going,' Jeanie asked her husband.

James unrolled the large map he had with him on the table and they sat, one on either side, to look at it.

'Here we are at Sydney,' said Jeanie, pointing to the east coast of Australia. 'Now, we sail northeast as far as the Loyalty Islands. Then where do we go then?'

Her husband looked at the map. 'From the Loyalty Islands we sail just north of due east to Niue because we have cargo to take there.'

'So we pass Fiji to the north and sail through the Tongan islands.'

'That's right,' agreed James. 'And from Niue we sail northeast to Samoa then turn south east for the final sail to Rarotonga.'

'And home,' his wife sighed. 'On the map the distances don't look very far but Rarotonga is almost half-way to South America.'

James laughed. 'Not quite! But who knows? If we lose our way we might find ourselves bathing on Chile's sandy beaches!'

All went well until January, when the *John Williams* was preparing to set sail from Niue for Samoa. Most of the passengers had gone ashore to visit a missionary there and the islanders prepared to give them a kindly send-off. Some came with great hands of bananas, others with armfuls of coconuts and yams and taro. There seemed to be no end of the gifts they were being given. In late afternoon James and his wife went with some of their fellow passengers by small boat out to their ship, the remainder agreeing to follow in the morning.

'There's quite a swell,' Captain Williams said. 'But we're far enough from land to be safe.'

'Why's the ship drifting astern?' the Mate asked. 'The current seems to be in the opposite direction.'

The missionaries and some others were just about to have evening prayers when the call went out for all hands on deck.

'What's happening?' Jeanie asked, when her husband had a minute to speak to her.

'The Captain has given orders that the whaleboat be lowered to take us in tow. We're drifting dangerously far and fast?

Another boat was lowered and a towline fastened to it too, but still the *John Williams* drifted astern. Yet another boat, a gig, was put out to help in the towing operation. But the sailing ship drifted faster than ever towards the shore! James and the other Christians on board prayed for the boat to be saved, and as they prayed the crew battled against the sea.

'Take soundings!' Captain Williams ordered.

Soundings were taken but no bottom found.

'Fire the rockets!'

Flares shot into the air to warn those on shore that the ship was in danger.

'What good will that do?' someone cried. 'No boat would brave this swell to come for us. I've never seen anything like it. It's as though the sea is on the boil!'

'How far are we from the reef and the shore?' Captain asked.

'Not far enough,' the Mate said heavily. 'And though the soundings are not showing the bottom we'll hit it soon enough if we don't change direction.'

'How many are on board?' shouted Captain Williams.

'About 70. We should get some of them off if we can. It will lighten the ship and save their lives at least.'

'If they get to shore!' worried the Captain. 'Get the gig alongside.'

The Mate did what he needed to do. Only the women and children were helped into the gig and it moved a safe distance away. Then the other two towing boats were cut loose and took their share of passengers, James among them. All three boats lay off to see what would happen to the brave ship.

'Look at that!' yelled one of the men.

The *John Williams* seemed to be suspended in the air!
CRASH!!!!!!!!!!
The sea sucked the ship down with a roar on to the reef.

'She's breaking up!'

'She's going under!'

People in the three boats watched horrified as their home for many months shattered in front of their eyes. With each surge of the sea more ship's timbers flew into the air. Sails ripped from top to bottom as the masts were thrust apart by the sheer force of it all. Those manning the three boats moved them back towards the shore out of the way of the debris that threatened to smash into them.

'She's gone!' a voice said quietly, and strangely, in the midst of the storm and the surge of the sea, there was a great quietness like the quietness that comes with a death.

The *John Williams* had gone.

For passengers and crew alike Nuie became home until another ship could be found to take them on their onward voyage.

'What are they doing?' James asked, as he and Jeanie walked along the shore one day soon afterwards.

'I've no idea,' she laughed. 'But it looks dangerous.'

The couple stopped to watch what the young folk were about.

'Look at him! He seems to be running into the sea with a plank of wood. Now he's jumping on to it on the crest of a wave and ... he's letting himself be washed ashore on the enormous surf that's thrown in from the reef! That's very clever!'

Jeanie looked at her husband and wondered about his sanity!

'It's called surf-swimming,' James told her a few days later, having discussed the sport with some Niue islanders who spoke a little English.

For a week that part of the shore was James's favourite walk as he studied surf-swimming techniques.

'I think I could do that,' he said to himself. 'And it looks really exciting.'

Two more days of watching the sport were enough to tempt James to try.

'I nearly lost my life,' he wrote to a friend some time later. 'One day the sea was particularly big and I decided to try and run in with a plank. I got too far out and was sucked back against some huge boulders that cut and bruised me badly. I thought I was lost when a great wave caught me and threw me right on to a boulder. It was then or never. I clung to it with all my strength and stayed there until someone saw me and came to my rescue. I was in bed several days with my injuries … and I've not tried surf-swimming again!'

Eventually those who had been shipwrecked were picked up and taken to Samoa on the *Rona*. Having left England on 4th January 1866, they arrived at their mission field on 20th May, 1867. The journey had taken one year, four months and sixteen days!

'What fellow name belong you?' James, who was first to be taken ashore, was asked by an islander.

'Chalmers,' he replied.

The Rarotongan who had asked the question did his best to repeat the strange-sounding foreign name.

'Tamate!' the man said, by way of introduction, when he showed the newcomer to his friends. And Tamate became the name by which James was known thereafter.

'Now,' said Jeanie, as soon as they had begun to be settled. 'Tell me some facts and figures about Rarotonga that would interest our friends who are praying for us.'

'I can tell you that all right,' Tamate said. 'We're 600 miles southwest of Tahiti, in 21 degrees south latitude and

160 degrees west longitude. And Rarotonga is the largest island of the Hervey Group.'

'James!' laughed Jeanie. 'I'm writing to friends not sailors or scientists. Tell me what you think they'd be interested in hearing.'

'Ah,'Tamate laughed. 'That's a bit different. How about telling them that the island is encircled by an outer reef 35 miles in circumference ... which makes it ideal for surf-swimming ....'

'Don't you even think about it!' his wife said. 'What else is there to say about Rarotonga?'

'You could mention that its mountains go up to about 3000 feet or 1000 metres, that the reef is made of coral and is from a quarter of a mile to half a mile broad. And they might get some idea of the dangers of a reef if you were to explain that at low tide it's well above water level and at high tide it's four to six feet below the surface.'

'I'm not sure that I need to explain how dangerous a reef is,' Jeanie laughed. 'My last letter to them described the sinking of the *John Williams* on the reef at Niue! I think they might have got the message.'

'Then you could tell them that there are two breaks in the Rarotongan reef, one on the north side of the island and one on the southeast side, and that smallish boats can get through them at high tide. But you'd better not mention the miles and miles of silver sandy beaches or our friends will think we've just come here for a holiday!'

'It's so good to have you in Avarua,' said Mr Krause. 'My wife and I have been missionaries here for some time. But I have been ill and your coming will allow me to have a break and recover.'

'I'm supposed to be working at Ngatangiia, on the other side of the island,' Tamate reminded him. 'But I'll do what I can to help you out here in Avarua.'

Very soon Tamate and Jeanie discovered their plans were changed. Mr Krause felt strongly that they should remain in Avarua rather than going on to Ngatangiia, at least for a time. And it was there that Tamate and Jeanie had their first taste of Rarotongan mission work.

'What's that noise?' asked Mr Krause one morning shortly afterwards.

'Look!' said Jeanie. 'Look outside!'

A crowd of Rarotongans were marching towards the mission house!

'Thump, thump, thump,' went their bare feet, as they marched in unison.

A chant set up that made Mr and Mrs Krause very nervous.

'Some of them are dancing!' Jeanie told her husband. 'They look as though they mean business. Do you think they're being friendly or not?'

'I don't know,' said Tamate. 'But Mr and Mrs Krause don't look too happy.'

'Thump! Thump! Thump!' the noise was louder than ever as the crowd marched on the spot outside the mission station.

Being unfamiliar with the local people, Jeanie couldn't tell whether they were coming in welcome or in war. In her mind she could hear the words Mrs Krause had spoken the previous evening. 'War, either offensive or defensive, is their continual employment and delight.'

'Was this war?' Jeanie asked herself. 'Was this how

wars were started in Rarotonga?'

A chant began at the front of the crowd then worked its way backwards.

'We want our missionary!' they shouted. 'We want our missionary!'

'What're they saying?' demanded Tamate.

Mr Krause looked worried to the point of fear.

'They want you,' he said. 'They're demanding their missionary. They must have come from Ngatangiia and they want to take you back with them.'

Tamate relaxed and smiled.

'That's fine,' he said. 'We'll go back with them for a visit then return to do the work here until we're free to go over there again.'

'But you don't understand,' pleaded Mr Krause. 'I recognise some Christians among them but there will be others too, others who might want you for evil reasons.'

'What are you saying?' Jeanie asked.

The older missionary wiped the sweat from his forehead. His wife stood silent, not knowing quite what to say.

Mr Krause took a deep breath. 'There are still cannibals on Ngatangiia,' he said. 'And they are more than capable of coming here in the crowd just to get you away from the safety of Avarua.'

'And?' asked Tamate.

'And they'll try to separate you from the others on the way to Ngatangiia. I just can't take the responsibility of letting you go with them. You've no idea what might happen. You're new here. You don't know the dangers you might face.'

'Then I'll take the decision, not you,' Tamate said

firmly. 'We'll go with them and we'll be back to help in the work here as soon as we possibly can.'

'But ...'

'Jeanie, get ready to go.'

The two young Scots left the mission house and walked into the crowd where they were welcomed with outstretched arms. Some men brought forward the contraptions they had made to carry their missionaries home to Ngatangiia, two simple chairs lashed to polls. Jeanie and Tamate were hoisted on to them, and with a bearer at each end of their chair-poles the young couple were lifted to shoulder height. Without wasting a single minute, those who were carrying them broke into a run and ran with their burdens in the direction of Ngatangiia.

Jeanie looked back and saw Mrs Krause's anxious face. She knew exactly what the older woman was thinking. Would they ever meet again? Had they come all the way to Rarotonga to be captured by cannibals as soon as they were out of sight of the safety of Avarua? Had they spent one year, four months and sixteen days travelling from Britain to this South Sea Island just to be eaten?

Rarotonga

'I think you can let me walk now,' Tamate said to his bearers when they were well out of the village. 'There's no need to carry me.'

Pleased that their new missionary had learned some of their language, the four men lowered him to the ground. Suddenly a crowd surrounded him and Jeanie lost sight of her husband. For a split second she was overcome with fear. 'You brought us here,' she said to the Lord. 'And I know you're with us.' The fear left her as she realised that those with whom they were travelling were friendly and welcoming, even if they showed it in rather a different way from what she was used to!

The days Tamate and Jeanie spent at Ngatangiia passed quickly because they felt happy and at home there.

'Why do you have to go back to Avarua?' the people asked. 'We need you here.'

'I know,' explained Tamate. 'But it's not for long. It's just to help Mr and Mrs Krause until they leave for home.'

'We need you,' pleaded a young man. 'We need you to teach us so that we can teach our people about Jesus.'

'People everywhere need to know about Jesus,' said Tamate.

'I know that,' the young man agreed, 'but there are people in Rarotonga who are very wicked.'

Jeanie and Tamate had heard about cannibalism for as

long as they'd heard about missionaries, but it had always been at a safe distance. Were they now going to hear of things happening close to their new home?

'Listen to me,' said the young man urgently. 'Let me tell you what my people do.'

Nodding for him to go on, Tamate prepared for a hard lesson. He didn't know quite how hard it would be.

'The people of Rarotonga live in tribes,' said the young man. 'And the tribes war against each other all the time. If ever a tribe is not at war it's because it's planning a really big one.'

'What are the wars about?' Jeanie asked.

'Village boundaries mostly, or revenge for something that's been done. But they don't really need a reason to fight. For them to live is to fight. They live by fighting and for fighting. When the men are too old to fight they lie down and die.'

Another Rarotongan sat down close by and joined in the conversation.

'In some villages here the first men captured in a battle are sometimes still sacrificed to their gods,' he explained. 'Their heads are cut off and their bodies are eaten.'

'So cannibalism still happens here?' Tamate asked. 'I wondered about that.'

'Yes,' said the villager. 'It still happens occasionally, even though the people have heard about Jesus. But it doesn't happen when people truly believe in him.'

'I should hope not,' said Tamate. 'We change when we believe in Jesus.'

'Some things have to change,' pointed out the young man. 'When I believed in Jesus I had two daughters. Then I had another two daughters. If I hadn't been a Christian

I might have abandoned the two last daughters because I don't need them.'

An older man, Maretu, came over to the little group who were speaking.

'Tamate,' he said. 'Please come and be welcome to my home.'

Maretu was the pastor in Ngatangiia, and he more than most wanted the missionaries to stay there.

'So we must go back to Avarua,' concluded Tamate, after he'd explained the situation to the kind and gentle Maretu that evening.

'I understand,' said the pastor. 'We will pray for you working there and we will look for you coming back.'

A few days later Maretu walked to Avarua with the young couple. And by the time Tamate and Jeanie arrived at the Krause's home they knew they had found a friend.

'You are safe!' wept Mrs Krause. 'We've been so worried. We thought you might have ....'

She was unable to finish her sentence.

'We're quite safe,' Jeanie assured her. 'The trip to Ngatangiia went well and we're back just as we said we would be.'

Six weeks later the Krause family left for home and Tamate was in charge of the mission work in Rarotonga. Although he had genuinely hoped to move back to Ngatangiia and base his work there, it soon became clear that they should stay where they were. That was where the biggest church was and the training college too. Sad though it made him to think that he would not be living and working with Maretu, that decision had to be made.

The weeks that followed set the pattern for the next ten years. Tamate looked after the church, much as he would have done wherever it was in the world. He taught in the college, showing chiefs how to lead their people as well as his students how to teach their villagers about Jesus. Jeanie taught the women and girls and Tamate looked after the boys' school. Teaching and preaching could have taken up all of his time, but it was not allowed to do so. As the islanders knew that their missionary had some medical training, they brought him all sort of injuries to cope with: broken arms and legs, snake bites and countless fighting wounds. Jeanie looked after sick babies and worked with mothers who needed help with their children. It wasn't long before Tamate and his wife had quite a reputation in Rarotonga.

'I'm glad those troublemakers are staying on the other side of the island,' said an angry Rarotongan who lived in the village of Ngatangiia. 'If they'd come here they'd just have stirred things up.'

'You're right there!' his friend agreed. 'I don't suppose they'd have approved of tonight's entertainment.'

Carrying a cask of orange beer between them, the two men headed for their favourite clearing in the woods.

'We'll get the fire going!' one of them shouted back to a group of men in the village. 'See you later!'

As darkness fell their campfire glowed, then blazed, then became more of a bonfire than a campfire. The firelight gave a dramatic edge to the scene as ones and twos and small groups of men arrived.

A voice yelled from the darkness of the woods as an already drunk teenager appeared.

There was something sinister about the gathering even then, but as the night wore on things went from bad to worse.

There was one thing these young men wanted, and one thing only. Alcohol. Yelling and screaming for beer, a thug lashed out with his fist at someone who tried to steer him away from the fire. He screeched, punching his helper who fell headlong, landing with his feet in the edge of the fire.

Someone grabbed his victim by the shoulders and hauled him away from the red hot embers. Someone else poured a gourd of water over him and left him to suffer his burns! Soon the only sober person there was the man who was burnt and not one of his companions cared a stick. By the early hours of the morning a great fight was in progress.

'Take that!' spat a Rarotongan, thumping out at whoever was beside him. It didn't seem to matter to him who he hit.

The man next to him turned round and, breaking a low branch off a tree, he whacked his assailant mightily on the back of the head. Drunken brawls occurred throughout the whole night and it took the first weak light of morning to expose the damage.

'We couldn't have had a good night like that if those busybodies lived in Ngatangiia,' one of the worst of the men said the next evening.

His brother, who had been burned in the fire, wasn't quite so sure.

On the other side of the island Tamate had heard about just such a gathering in the forest near Avarua.

'Next time they have a drunken orgy they'll get more than they bargained for,' he told Jeanie.

'Why?' she asked. 'What are you going to do?'

'I'll know when the time comes,' her husband smiled. 'There are some things you can't plan in detail in advance!'

Tamate didn't have long to wait. He watched for the signs: the brewing of orange beer, the secret conversations, the trips into the forest. He watched. He listened. And, because he knew more of the language than the young men realised, they were sometimes brazenly careless in their talk.

'It's tonight,' he told Jeanie one day. 'And they're in for a big surprise.'

'You'll be careful, won't you?' she asked.

And her words might as well have wafted into thin air for all the impact they made on Tamate.

The drunken orgy near Avarua followed much the same awful pattern as the one on the other side of the island. Having let the young men have an hour or so on their own, Tamate set out into the wood to find the clearing in which they had gathered.

As he drew near the din was so great that he didn't need to use his eyes to see where he was going. For dramatic effect Tamate stood behind bushes at the edge of the clearing, just where the firelight shone brightest. Then, when a noise had all the young men looking in his direction, he thrust the branches apart and stood glaring at them. It was just as well that Tamate didn't know any Rarotongan swear words because he would not have been pleased at what was said all round the bonfire when the drunken young men saw who was there!

Tamate, without a single shiver of fear, strode out into the middle of the clearing to the orange beer barrel. With one great thud he knocked a hole in its side and watched as the beer poured out on to the ground below. The firelight reflected in the liquor so that every single man present could see it disappearing into the earth. They looked like balloons that had been pricked with pins.

'Now,' said Tamate, 'Let's sit down and talk.'

He sat on a tree stump and waited. Amazed, and a little in awe, the men eventually sat down on the ground or on nearby branches or trees.

'You think this is how to enjoy yourself,' the missionary said. 'Well, let me tell you a much better way than this.'

Tamate looked round about him at the angry and puzzled faces highlit by the bonfire. Would they listen to what he had to tell him?

Amazed at the missionary's courage, the young men did listen. And, after Tamate had gone away, and after the beer had thoroughly dried into the ground, they talked over what had happened.

'He says that we can be happy without orange beer?'

'Do you believe him?'

'Phew! I've tried everything, and the only thing that makes me happy is beer.'

'He says Jesus can make us happy.'

'That's rubbish. Don't believe a word he says. He's just trying to get your money for the church.'

'Don't be stupid! He didn't even mention money!'

'Well, you listen to him if you like. I know where there's orange beer that he doesn't know anything about.'

Some of the men stalked off in search of more to drink. Others stood around and talked.

Tamate, who listened to their voices carrying in the night air as he walked through the woods home, wondered if any would accept his invitation to come to hear about Jesus. It was in Christ alone that they would find true happiness.

'I think I'd like to do some exploring today,' he told Jeanie the next afternoon. 'My mind's not very alert after last night's little adventure.'

'An afternoon off would do you good,' she said. 'What are you thinking of doing?'

'I'd love to go out and explore the reef,' said Tamate. 'The tide's about right. I should be able to get out of the boat and on to the reef in an hour or so.'

He went in search of some men to go with him.

Just as the reef began to break the surface of the water he and several Rarotongans skimmed across the lagoon in a boat.

'What are you doing?' one asked, as Tamate stood up in the prow of the boat.

'I'm going on to the reef to see what it's like,' he said, making a jump for it.

As he jumped the boat grounded on the reef. Tamate, thinking he was going to land on solid coral, discovered that only water was under his feet! The reef at that point was narrower than he had estimated and he overshot the far side of it!

'Help!' he yelled, as he slid down the side of the reef and was caught in the undercurrent.

Throwing his oar down, one of his companions leapt on to the coral and made a grab for Tamate's arm. The current was dragging him down and the waves from the open sea did their best to push him under.

'Hold on!' hissed his rescuer through gritted teeth. 'Hold on for all you're worth.'

The two men gripped each other's wrists as though life depended on it. It did.

Between them the strong islanders managed to pull their missionary on to the reef then into the boat.

'That was a close thing!' one of the Rarotongans said, as they paddled through the lagoon and headed for the sandy shore.

'I must still have work to do for the Lord here,' the Scot smiled weakly and wetly.

'Maybe you should stay on dry land then,' his companions suggested.

'Being a missionary here is very different from what I imagined,' Tamate complained to his wife. 'It's almost like being a minister at home.'

'Excuse me,' Jeanie smiled. 'I don't remember you going to midnight drunken orgies in the woods around Inveraray. Nor do I remember you nearly drowning off a coral reef or being carried around on a chair by four strong bearers.'

'No,' laughed her husband. 'You're right enough. But I was once washed away in a herring box at Ardrishaig!'

Jeanie grinned. 'I don't want to know,' she said. 'I don't want to know.'

'I've just had a thought,' said Tamate, pretending to be serious. 'The surf from the reef when the tide comes in would be great for surf-swimming!'

Vainemuri

'You have no idea how often I bump into that monstrosity!' announced Tamate, as he pushed past the ancient, and very dead, printing press in the mission house. 'The only good thing it does is hold the floor down.'

'It is a brute of a contraption,' Jeanie agreed. 'It's a pity it couldn't be put to use.'

That sent her husband's mind ticking over … always a dangerous thing!

'I've an idea!' he said just a few days afterwards.

'Let me sit down and brace myself,' Jeanie laughed. 'I've met your ideas before now.'

'If I could get that printing press working again we could print a newspaper for Rarotonga!'

Jeanie thought about it for a minute before agreeing that it was one of her husband's better ideas, better at least than falling off a coral reef into the open sea!

'I take it this wouldn't be a daily paper?'

'No,' Tamate replied. 'But I think we could print something monthly. It all depends on whether or not I can make this brute work for a living.'

Every spare minute of the days that followed was spent dismantling the printing press, cleaning each large and little part of it, then building it back together again.

'Look!' said Tamate when the job was done. 'I've no bits left over! Let's do a trial run.'

And that trial run was a success! The missionary had a new job. He was now Tamate: missionary, minister, teacher, health worker and repairer of elderly printing presses!

'I've decided to start a monthly island newspaper,' he told the people in church and in the training college.

'What do we want a newspaper for?' some asked. 'We don't need news. We know all we need to know.'

Others were more open-minded. 'What would you put in the newspaper?' they asked.

Tamate had already thought about that. 'It would have news from the various parts of Rarotonga, give shipping reports, letters from islanders, articles on subjects of interest and perhaps give readings from books you'd find interesting. And when ships come in we could add news from other countries of the world.'

'I like the idea of letters from islanders,' someone said. 'I could write about those awful people in the village on the hill who are always stealing my yams.'

Within weeks of the idea coming into his mind the first newspaper was printed, and it came out on the first of each month thereafter.

One month the paper carried news of a sickness that threatened to become an epidemic on Rarotonga. Before long people in village after village developed the sickness and many of them died.

'Vainemuri's got the sickness,' Jeanie was told by an anxious member of the church.

'I'm so sorry,' she replied. 'But Vainemuri's a fine fourteen-year-old girl. She may be strong enough to fight it off.'

As she made the meal that night Jeanie thought of the sick girl. 'She's such a good quiet girl,' she said to herself. 'And she never misses a Sunday at church or a day at school. In fact, she's a real example to the other girls her age.'

'Vainemuri's very poorly,' was the next news that was heard.

Tamate and Jeanie went together to visit the sick teenager, who knew by then that she was likely to die.

'Don't worry about me,' said Vainemuri. 'And don't be sorry for me because I'm going home to Jesus.'

'That's what she tells all her friends who come to see her,' said Vainemuri's mother, as the missionary couple left. 'But I still hope that she doesn't die.'

Jeanie put her arm round the poor woman. 'I hope so too,' she said. 'But it may be that this is God's time to take her home.'

A short time later Tamate visited Vainemuri's home once again. The girl was very weak and unable to speak.

'Would you like me to read to you from the Bible?' he asked.

Vainemuri nodded her head weakly and smiled.

The missionary read some verses about heaven then prayed quietly, asking for God's will to be done. The next day, as the sun set in the evening, Vainemuri closed her eyes for the very last time on earth and her soul went straight to heaven.

'We'll miss her such a lot. Vainemuri was a really special girl,' Tamate told one of the elders in the church after the funeral.

'Let me tell you what happened just the other day,' said the old man. 'I went to see the child and I asked her if she held firmly to Christ. She opened her eyes and told me, "He holds me and I cling to him." Then I asked her if she was afraid. She smiled at the question and said, "No, I shall see Jesus. I love him."'

As the old man told Tamate this story the tears ran down his face. And as he listened to it the missionary wiped a tear from his own eye. There were many sad people in the village that day but Vainemuri was not among them. She was in perfect joy and peace in heaven.

Of course, there were times when the missionaries themselves were unwell, and they coped in very different ways.

'Jeanie keeps the very best of health,' Tamate wrote home on several occasions. And he thought it was true. But the real truth was that when Jeanie was unwell she struggled on and pretended there was nothing whatever wrong. It was very rare indeed for her to have to admit to sickness. Tamate had quite a different way of coping. Blessed with good health and strength, if he was unwell for a while, as soon as he felt able to do so he climbed one of the highest hills in Rarotonga!

'The climb does me good,' he said. 'The cooler air at the top does me more good, and the view does me best of all.'

Vainemuri's home was not the only one that Tamate and Jeanie went to visit together. In fact, the pair of them set out to visit the entire island, as he explained to a friend.

'We made up a plan of visitation in which we visited every house in each of the settlements. The island pastor of each settlement and his wife accompanied us. We read the Bible and prayed in every home before leaving. I always asked the people we were visiting if I could use their Bible for the reading. In that way I discovered if they had a Bible and if it was well read or covered with dust! It's a pleasure to think that there's not a home on the island in which we have not shared the Word of God.'

As time went on Tamate believed more and more that Rarotonga should be looked after by local pastors rather than by missionaries. At least there many homes possessed a Bible even if it was never read. The training school had also produced some fine men and he felt it was time that the two western missionaries moved on.

'I've always wanted to work where people have never heard the name of Jesus,' he told Jeanie, who knew very well that was the case.

'If God wants us to move from here,' she said, 'he'll make it clear when the time comes.'

The time did come, eventually, after ten years of serving the Rarotongans. And Tamate and Jeanie left the people they had come to love and sailed to Papua New Guinea. Once again Jeanie looked out the map to check exactly where they were going.

'I didn't realise that the southernmost tip of Papua New Guinea was quite as near the northernmost tip of Australia,' she said. 'Only the Torres Straits separate the two countries.'

'Much more than the Torres Straits separate them,'

Tamate corrected her. 'Australia is a civilised country. Papua New Guinea is probably one of the most uncivilised countries in the whole world.'

'It's a huge island,' Jeanie commented. 'From the map it looks about three times the size of Britain.'

'But while in Britain nearly everyone speaks English, though Gaelic and Welsh are spoken by some, in Papua New Guinea there seems to be hundreds of different languages, and I do mean different.'

'How has that come about?' his wife wondered.

'I think it has a lot to do with the terrain. There are massively high mountains, four times higher than anything here in Rarotonga, separated by deep narrow gorges. So two villages could be just a few miles apart but have a mountain range or an impassable gorge between them.'

'It doesn't sound the easiest place to reach with the good news about Jesus,' said Jeanie thoughtfully.

'No,' agreed Tamate, his eyes shining with excitement, 'But it's where God is calling us and it's where we want to be.'

Jeanie smiled. She was no less an adventurer than her husband, and this sounded like the adventure of a lifetime. Until five years before the land was nearly unknown and unexplored. When the two Scots arrived, the population was almost totally ignorant about the Lord Jesus Christ.

In a letter to a friend in Britain Jeanie described her impression of their new home after she'd been there just a short time.

'The people in this part of the island (we're on the southeast coast) are light-coloured,' she wrote, 'not dark like the Africans. Many wear little or nothing apart from sticks through their noses, earrings through gaping holes in their ear lobes, necklaces and feathers. In fact, some of their bodies are so covered in paint and tattoos that at first you're not aware that they have no clothes on!'

'Write about their homes,' said Tamate, when he read the beginning of the letter.

Jeanie took up her pen and continued.

'Their homes are mostly made of palm leaves and wood planks and contain no furniture at all, unless you call a plank of wood furniture. Many are built on stilts as much of the land is swampy. I think they sometimes sleep on planks of wood on the floor. I've not seen a table or chair or any other piece of what we would call furniture in any of the villages we've visited. The interesting thing is that people don't live as though they are poor because they don't know that anyone anywhere lives any differently from they do. In fact, they look at us as though we come from the moon!'

Among the Christian workers in Papua New Guinea were two couples from Rarotonga, Ruatoka and his wife and Piri and his wife.

'Tell me about yourself,' Tamate asked Piri, when they first met.

The islander smiled. 'I was very fond of orange beer,' the man admitted, 'so fond of it that I hated the missionaries for telling us it was evil. Once, when I was really drunk, I set out to kill the missionary. Thankfully, some people heard me saying what I was going to do and they followed me, captured me, tied me up and dragged me home. When I'd sobered up I was so horrified that I'd nearly killed a man that I swore I'd never drink orange beer again. After that I started going to church and then I became a Christian.

Now I tell everyone I meet about the Lord Jesus, though many don't want to know. They do all sorts of things to stop us telling people the Gospel.'

Shortly afterwards Tamate discovered that for himself.

'Let's get organised so that we can leave as soon as the tide suits,' Piri suggested, when they were going on a mission trip together.

They went to bed and slept till morning.

'The tide will be right soon,' Piri told Tamate. 'I think we should get ready.'

The two men went with their crew down to the boat and climbed aboard. They were going to visit a village further along the coast.

'Where are the rowlocks?' one of the crew asked.

There wasn't a rowlock on the boat. Each oar was just resting on the side!

'They've been stolen,' moaned Piri. 'Someone doesn't want us to go out preaching!'

Climbing out of the boat, Piri told the headman that they wanted the rowlocks back, and quickly!

'Nobody has them,' the headman said, when he'd gone through the village.

Piri, determined to find them, stalked between the houses. 'Nobody will leave this place until every house has been searched and the rowlocks found!'

Before the serious search started a woman appeared beside the boat.

'I found these in the street,' she said, handing the rowlocks to Piri.

The other Rarotongan, Ruatoka, was well known to Tamate and Jeanie as he had trained in the mission college while they were there. Along with some others he had gone to Papua New Guinea ahead of the Scots and had done good work there. He and his wife were kind-hearted and always looked for ways of helping people.

Not long after Tamate and Jeanie arrived, a large number of Australian prospectors sailed to Papua New Guinea looking for gold. Their base was Port Moresby, where Ruatoka and his wife lived.

'I heard a rumour that some inland tribes are going to attack the prospectors,' Ruatoka told his wife. 'Those tribes are cannibals and I don't even want to think what might happen if they attack.'

'What can you do about it?' she asked.

'I'll take one or two Christians with me and we'll warn the Australians of the danger they're in.'

Leaving his wife virtually running the hospital at Port Moresby single-handedly, Ruatoka marched inland with his companions.

'The rumour is that the tribes are meeting at Moumiri. We should head there after we've put the gold-diggers on their guard,' he told his men.

Having warned the prospectors of the danger, Ruatoka and the others continued their march to Moumiri. They were jumped on, and things looked deadly serious.

'Why do you want to kill me?' Ruatoka asked. 'What have I done?'

The Christian talked with the tribesmen, prayed for them and told them about Jesus. One by one the painted warriors went back to their villages, leaving the gold-diggers to get on with their work. When Tamate told his wife what had happened, he finished by saying, 'That's the kind of people we've come to, Jeanie. And that's the kind of danger we're in.'

The Rainmaker

'So much of this island has never been reached for Jesus,' Tamate said to another missionary. 'I think we should work in different places and meet different people.'

Mr Lawes, who had been in Papua New Guinea for four years when the Scots arrived, agreed that would be a good idea. 'Let's sail along the coast and look for suitable sites for mission stations.'

Tamate and his wife (who by then was known as Tamate Vaine) along with Mr Lawes set off east, rowed by strong crewmen who never seemed to tire of the sea.

'Let's have a look around here,' suggested Tamate, as they neared an area of mangrove swamp near a village.

They all clambered out the boat and set off to explore.

'What are they?' Jeanie asked, pointing at some unusual trees.

'They're sago palms,' she was told.

Tamate picked up a strange-looking seed. 'Look at this,' he said.

'Stop!' yelled an islander, grabbing it from him. 'If you eat that you'll swell up...' As the man spoke he held out his hands to show that Tamate would swell up like a gigantic balloon if he ate the seed.

'Thank you very much,' said Jeanie gratefully. 'We don't want him that size!'

'Or dead,' added Mr Lawes.

No suitable site for a mission station was found that day

and many trips were made in search of good places.

'That looks interesting,' Tamate said, pointing from the boat to a village on a wooded point. Let's investigate.'

The crew turned in the direction of the village and pulled their oars.

'Yeiewew!!!!!!' shrieked a man who was fishing nearby.

'That poor fellow's terrified!' said Tamate. 'He'll never have seen a white man before and he probably thinks I'm some kind of evil spirit. Give me something to hold out as a gift.'

Jeanie scrabbled about in the baggage and took out a piece of red cloth and some beads.

'Go alongside slowly,' said Tamate, 'and I'll hold these out to him.'

The closer they moved the more awful the man looked. Jeanie wondered if she was seeing things, but she was not. It *was* a human jawbone the wild-looking man wore on his arm for decoration! Putting all thoughts of how he came about such a treasure, Jeanie picked up the knitting she always carried with her and got on with it. She might be in the presence of a cannibal but her husband still needed socks!

Carrying the gifts he'd been given, the fisherman paddled like fury for the shore to show them off. Within minutes of his arriving in the village several canoes were on their way out. Some islanders clambered on to the deck of Tamate's boat and one of them, his name was Kirikeu, sat down beside Jeanie and watched her knitting!

'Goodness me,' she thought, glancing to the side at her companion. 'What an interesting old man!'

Studying the visitor, she noted his appearance carefully in order to describe him when she next wrote home.

'He's wearing a necklace of bones and his arms are

decorated with shells. At least that's preferable to a human jawbone! And he has the most enormous feathers stuck into his hair!'

The next day Kirikeu was back. He'd decided he liked this very odd white woman who tied knots in strange creepers with two straight sticks!

'This is for you,' he said in his own language, giving fruit to Jeanie.

'He's a fine old man despite appearances,' decided Tamate. 'I'll try to persuade him to act as our guide.'

Kirikeu was delighted, and before long he had shown them a good place to build a house on the little island of Suau. The idea of a mission station didn't mean anything to him whatever.

'There's fresh water here,' said Kirikeu. 'And the mainland is just a short distance away.'

'But where will we live until our new home is built?' asked Jeanie.

Tamate, with Kirikeu's help, hatched a plan. They would live in half of the headman's house in exchange for some beads, tomahawks and pieces of cloth.

When the headman saw Jeanie's reaction to his décor, he explained. 'My people are cannibals. That's why we have such a good collection of human skulls.'

'I can see that,' the woman agreed. And as she looked at the other end of his home she found an amazing array of black wooden spears, clubs with heads made of stone and brightly painted shields decorated with feathers.

'So this is home for a while,' she thought. 'It's certainly different!'

Building proceeded on the mission house with the help of the villagers who were happy to work for cloth, knives and other things with which Tamate paid them.

'What's that noise?' the missionary asked one day, when he was working on the shore.

Looking up he saw that there was a raid and the headman's house was surrounded by a violent mob of painted men. Racing up to the village, he pushed his way into the crowd, jumped up on to the platform of the house and demanded to know what they wanted! One of them, the fiercest of the men, rushed at Tamate with his stone-headed club raised to strike him.

'What do you want?' the Scot demanded loudly.

'Knives, tomahawks and iron!' the warrior spat. 'Give us them or I'll kill you.'

'I will not!' Tamate said firmly. 'You may kill me but I most certainly am not giving weapons to people who are already armed to the teeth!'

'Give them something,' hissed one of the teachers who was working with Tamate. 'He really will kill you.'

Scowling at the warriors for their cheek, the missionary looked their leader straight in the eye. 'I never give gifts to people who are armed,' he said firmly, and walked away.

The raiders, shocked into utter confusion by his fearless response, slid into the darkness of the trees around the clearing.

'Tamate,' said Kirikeu next morning, when the missionary was preparing planks for building. 'This is the chief of the raiders. He's sorry for what happened yesterday.'

The Scot turned to look at Kirikeu's companion.

'You look better without all your paintwork,' said Tamate. 'And now that you aren't armed we can be friends.'

From the very first day they spent in the headman's house, Tamate had held services in the village. By the time of the raid several villagers had come to listen to what he had to say. And the day afterwards one or two of the raiders came to hear him! Underneath the tamano tree, where many a cannibal feast had been held, the Scottish missionary stood and told his hearers about the God of love.

'The house is finished now,' said Tamate. 'It's time to move in.'

Before she left the headman's home, Jeanie took one last look around.

'I'd like to ask you something,' she said to her husband.

'What's that?'

'When you're thinking about the decoration of our new home, I'd rather we had something a little less dramatic than human skulls, clubs and spears!'

The missionary couple looked at each other and laughed. Both knew that there would be no fancy decoration in their simple home, far less human remains and weapons. All their time and effort was spent in telling people about Jesus.

'I think we should organise a missionary expedition into the mountains,' Tamate said, after a short time in their new home on Suau. 'Will you be all right while I'm away.'

He looked at his wife, knowing that although she didn't complain she really wasn't as well as she might be.

'I'll be fine,' Jeanie said. 'The villagers call me the White Lady of Suau and they look after me so lovingly.'

'That's because they know you love them.'

'The mission teacher is kind to me too. Yes, you go. There's work to be done.'

Tamate and his companions headed for the mountains, carrying with them the good news that he knew the islanders needed to know. Jesus had come to be the Saviour of his people and only through him could anyone go to heaven. With that good news in his heart and his head the Scot climbed upwards from the swamplands through the forest.

'It's strange,' he thought as he climbed. 'Back home in Scotland you only need to climb 2000 feet above sea level and you're above the tree-line. Here trees grow right to the very top of 12,000 feet high mountains!'

From village to village Tamate went with his companions, his life often in danger. But when the people saw his fearlessness of their painted faces and their cannibalistic decorations they often stopped and listened to what he said.

'Are you not afraid of the spirits?' he was asked. 'Do you sacrifice to the evil spirits to stop them from harming you?'

'No,' said Tamate firmly. 'I worship the one true God, and his Holy Spirit is more powerful than any other spirit, and than all other spirits put together. He's my God and I've no need to fear.'

'The white man doesn't look afraid,' people whispered to each other.

Some young men gathered together to discuss the matter.

'Let's see if he's telling the truth,' they decided.

Painting themselves in the most ghastly possible way, they put on all the human bones and teeth they could find, even some human hair, and hid until dark. Then they crept up to where Tamate was telling stories about Jesus and howled like wolves! The missionary looked up into their furious contorted faces, then stared at their horribly painted bodies and deadly spears.

'Stop that din!' he shouted firmly. 'These people can't hear what I'm saying!'

'Tamate Vaine is not well,' a teacher said, as he went into the village one morning while Tamate was away.

'What's wrong with her?'

'She's sick. She can't eat and she's even whiter than usual.'

The people couldn't imagine anyone whiter than their beloved Tamate Vaine.

'Take this to her,' a woman said, handing the teacher a ripe mango.

'When will Tamate be back?' they wondered. 'Will he come soon enough?'

The villagers were confused. They knew what a Papua New Guinean looked like when he was dying. They knew the changes of skin colour to look for, the changes in the eyes. But they were completely at a loss with Jeanie. They didn't know what to expect.

'How is the White Lady of Suau,' the headman asked, when he met Kirikeu one morning.

The old man shook his head. 'She is whiter than whiteness. Yesterday she ate nothing. All she took was a little water. I wish Tamate would come.'

Day after day passed and the missionary didn't come.

'Where is he?' they asked each other.

Kirikeu looked up to the high mountains and pointed in their direction. 'That is where he is.'

'We'll go to look for him,' two young men said. The tension in the village was really getting at them. They could take the pressure of killing raids, but Jeanie's sickness was different. They didn't love those they fought against, but they did love the White Lady of Suau.

'Where will you look?' asked Kirikeu.

'The mountains,' said one of the young men eagerly.

Kirikeu raised his eyes and looked up at range upon range upon range of towering mountains. 'You would not know where to begin,' he said sadly. 'It would be like looking for a drop of water in the sea.'

'Tamate!' the shout went up, when the missionary returned home.

From every corner of the village people came running. They had heard the cry and they wanted to see him for themselves. He'd be able to help the White Lady of Suau, they were sure.

'Use this one!' said an elder, pulling his canoe into the water. 'I'll take you over.'

Tamate climbed in, as fearless of the future as ever, and was taken over the narrow stretch of water to his home.

'She'll be all right now,' the women told each other. 'Tamate will know how to make her better.'

When the Scot saw how poorly his wife was he knew that her only hope of real recovery was to go to Australia for treatment and rest.

'You'd get good medical care there,' he said, holding her in his arms.

'But I want to be here with you,' insisted Jeanie. 'I can't help you if I'm on the other side of the Torres Straits. In any case, I'm in no fit state to travel just now.'

Knowing the truth of that, Tamate relaxed and tenderly nursed his wife until she was well enough to travel. By then Jeanie knew herself that if she was ever to enjoy good health again she would need to go to Australia.

'Tamate Vaine will soon be back,' wept the women on the day she left.

In Sydney Jeanie had the best of attention. At first she seemed to grow stronger. But towards the end of 1878 she took a turn for the worse. And on 26th January a letter was brought to the village for Tamate. Knowing the handwriting was not his wife's, he opened it very slowly. What news might it contain?

'I'm sorry to have to tell you that your wife is seriously ill. I doubt that she will recover.' It was from one of the doctors who was caring for Jeanie.

Unable to leave Sueu immediately, Tamate did what he had to do, trusting his wife to God's care. It was several weeks before he was able to go.

'I think you should read this,' he was told in Cooktown on the northeast coast of Australia.

The speaker handed him a newspaper. Tamate glanced

at it, and there, in black and white, was the news that his beloved Jeanie had died.

'She's in heaven,' he told himself, as he walked on with his head bowed low. 'She's in heaven with Jesus.'

His mind flashed back over the years they'd been married.

'Jeanie's happier now that she's ever been,' he thought. 'And we have been happy together.'

His spirit rose a little as he reminded himself that the one he loved so much was safe home in heaven where there is no sickness, no pain, no death and no tears.

'I know that Jeanie's blissfully happy,' he said to himself. 'And I'm happy for her too.' A tear slid down his cheek. 'But I'm so sad for myself. How I'll miss her.'

'You should go home to Britain for a time,' people told him when he returned to Sueu. 'That would do you good.'

His mission teacher reminded Tamate that he had been planning to take Jeanie home for a while.

'I can't do that,' said the Scot. 'People would think I was running away from my work because I couldn't cope without my wife.'

Tamate thought long and hard about what he should do next.

'The work in Sueu is going really well,' he said, when he discussed it with the Christians there. 'I don't think I need to stay here now. Perhaps it's time I moved on and took the good news of Jesus Christ to another part of Papua New Guinea. Now that I don't need to think about Jeanie's health I can go to more dangerous places.'

The decision made, Tamate packed up his belongings and took a boat going along the coast to Port Moresby. It was a little while before he felt sure of what God wanted him to do. The missionary prayed, looked at maps, talked with other Christians, then began to pack.

On the evening of 15th July 1879, Ruatoka, the teacher whom Tamate had trained in mission work, wrote to a friend.

'Today I helped Tamate pack his things. He has gone off to the mountains. I wonder if I'll ever see him again before we meet in heaven.'

Wild pigs and wilder men

When Tamate travelled around the country visiting villages, meeting people and talking about the Lord Jesus, he took local men with him to carry all he needed.

'We're not going any further along this road,' his bearers announced one day as they travelled through the mountains. 'We've heard that there's a great pig in the forest, big enough to eat a man.'

'There are pigs everywhere in Papua New Guinea!' Tamate laughed. 'Every family has its own pig and none of them have eaten me yet!'

The bearers looked offended.

'This is not an ordinary pig. Perhaps it's the spirit of a ferocious creature and not even a pig after all.'

Tamate strode on in his usual way and his bearers had little choice but to follow him.

'They are wild-looking,' he agreed, when he saw the pigs in the village along the road. 'No wonder they've a bad reputation. They're the biggest and ugliest pigs I've ever seen.'

'Look out!' yelled a boy.

Tamate spun round and discovered an ugly brute of a pig, tusks down, charging in his direction! The bearers looked scared and amused at the very same time!

'Get away!' Tamate shouted at the animal, dodging it's razor-sharp tusks.

The pig stopped, turned and lowered his head for

another dash at his prey … but just then he caught sight of the village men closing in on him. With a toss of a grossly ugly head, he turned and strode away, tail in the air and grunting furiously!

'Why have you come to visit us?' the villagers asked when the pig had been put safely out of the way.

'I've come to tell you about the great and loving Spirit,' said Tamate.

'Spirits are not loving,' a boy said. 'We have to sacrifice to the spirits to stop them being spiteful and hurting us.'

'My God is a good Spirit,' the missionary went on. 'Would you like me to tell you about him?'

Used as they were to being terrified by the thought of evil spirits, the villagers were only too happy to hear about a Spirit who was not spiteful and evil.

'Would you like to have a teacher to live here in your village?' Tamate asked, when he'd finished speaking. 'He would teach you about the one true God who is good and loving.'

'Yes,' the people said, after a huddled discussion. 'We would like a teacher.'

Tamate took that as encouragement, though he wondered if they had heard about the gifts that teachers sometimes brought with them.

It was towards the end of November 1879 that Tamate, Piri and several others went by ship from Port Moresby to Boera.

'That's a strange ship,' the people said, pointing to its deck. 'Where are its sails? How does it move through the water at such speed?'

'It's a steam ship called the *Ellangowan*,' one of the crew explained. 'It has an engine that pushes it through the water.'

Men and women, boys and girls, came from miles around as the news travelled about this strange ship with something called an engine that made it go as if by magic.

From Boera they chugged along the coast to a district where the chief was Tamate's friend. Having lowered anchor, the missionary and some others skimmed across the water in canoes to the shore.

'Where's my friend Oa?' Tamate asked a villager.

The man shook his head. 'Oa is in the forest hunting. You will stay with us until he comes home.'

'They seem friendly,' thought the Scot, as the men greeted him in the traditional way, by rubbing noses with him!

By the time they had all rubbed noses, Tamate's face was covered in paint. The villagers had been painting themselves for a raid when he arrived!

'How many villages are there around here?' the Scot asked, wondering if it would be a suitable place to base a mission teacher.

'There are five along the shore,' he was told, 'and six others inland. None are far away from here. You should come with us to visit them.'

Thinking that was a good idea, he set out with a group of local men to explore. Small knots of women and children tagged along behind.

'This white man is a friend of Oa,' people were told in every village they visited, and Tamate had even more paint smudged on to his face in greeting!

As Oa did not return before the sun went down, the missionary decided to continue exploring further up the coast and come back again to see his friend. A few days later they were travelling parallel to the shore when several canoes were spied coming in their direction.

'The people of Karama are coming!' yelled one of the crew, recognising a warrior tribe on the move.

'They're armed to the teeth!' Tamate told the ship's Captain. 'Look at them. They've clubs, bows and arrows and goodness knows what all!'

The Captain nodded grimly. 'They're after blood all right. And we're nearly within reach of their arrows!'

'I am Tamate!' the Scot yelled out. 'And I come in peace.'

Bows were bent and arrows pointed in his direction. The captain of the *Ellangowan* held himself ready to give the command to get steam up. It seemed that the very air tingled with tension.

'I have gifts for you!' shouted Tamate.

The men slowly brought their canoes nearer the ship, but none of the warriors let their watch go down, or their bows and arrows. Holding the gifts over the side of the boat, the Scot looked down into the eyes of men he realised were killers, and men who fully intended to kill again ... soon. A quick warning glance at the Captain was passed on to the engineer and the *Ellangowan* began to move away, slowly at first then gathering speed.

'Full steam ahead!' ordered the Captain, as soon as they were just clear of the canoes.

The *Ellengowan* juddered into life and steamed away, tossing the canoes in its wake.

The warriors could move at speed through any waters, and they shot off in hot pursuit.

'They're following us!' the Captain said. 'Look at their speed!'

Arrows flew in their direction, some landing in the water just off the ship. But soon the arrows fell short of their mark, for even expert warrior oarsmen were no match for the steamship *Ellangowan*.

In the middle of the following summer Tamate was on the sea once again, this time to a place he knew there would be a friendly welcome. It took ten days to reach Maniumani on Redscar Bay where missionaries from Rarotonga had worked a few years before. Some of the Rarotongans had died and the remainder were moved to a healthier part of the country to work. The chief, whose name was Naimi, was sad about the missionaries moving away.

'What's wrong with you?' Tamate said, when he saw Naimi's unhappy face. 'Are you ill?'

'I'm not ill,' the old man said. 'Unless I'm ill with the sadness of not having a teacher here who can tell us about the Lord Jesus Christ.'

'You know what happened,' the Scot reminded his friend.

'I know I was first to welcome the teachers when they came to the village,' said Naimi. 'And I know that when the village warriors wanted to kill them I stopped it.'

Tamate looked at the old man sadly.

'I hear what you're saying, but your village is so swampy that disease is a terrible problem. That was why so many died just after they came and why it was thought best to take the others away.'

'You don't understand,' Naimi insisted. 'The year they came was a bad year everywhere. Our people died too. But that doesn't happen every year.' He was almost in tears. 'Will you not send me a teacher?'

Looking at the deep longing in his old friend's face, Tamate made a decision.

'I'm going on to another place where there are no disease-ridden swamps. It's a good place to stay and there's a teacher there. Will you come with me?'

Naimi's face lit up.

'The teacher will tell me about Jesus?' he asked, as if it was too good to be true.

'Yes,' said Tamate. 'You will learn from the teacher every day.'

There was no holding Naimi back. With the minimum of farewells he climbed aboard the boat and set out to learn more about Jesus.

News of Tamate's coming spread from village to village, and when his ship was seen steaming along the coast men set out in their canoes to pass on the message that he was coming. So his reputation went before him as he travelled along. On one occasion he and his colleagues arrived at a poor village where they were eaten alive by mosquitoes all night through. They'd put up nets to prevent them biting, but the cunning little creatures got underneath the mosquito nets and had a splendid feast on their visitors!

'What's that noise?' Tamate asked, first thing in the morning.

Opening his eyes, he discovered that the villagers had

been up for ages. They'd killed two pigs and tied them by their legs on to poles ready for cooking.

'The women have brought fruit and vegetables too,' his friend said. 'This looks like a regular feast!'

The cooking began, but Tamate felt uncomfortable as the local people kept making excuses to walk past him and look at his feet!

'Are toes a cannibal delicacy?' was a question that went through his mind several times that morning.

Then the whispering began.

'They must be part of his skin,' someone said, looking down at the missionary's strong boots.

'No,' a villager said. 'They can't be. His skin is white and his big feet are black. And see, he has no toes!'

The children who were listening to the conversation looked at their hands and feet and knew that Tamate was a very strange specimen indeed. His hands were one colour and his strange feet another! When Tamate realised what was interesting the villagers the missionary was both relieved and amused! They'd never seen boots before and they thought his boots were actually his feet!

As the feast went on fun and games, laughter and songs filled the air.

'Teach us a white man's song,' someone suggested.

Tamate thought back to Inveraray and the white man's song that is sung at feast times in Scotland. Holding hands with the person on each side of him, he began to sing '*Auld Lang Syne.*'

'Hold hands,' mothers told their children.

'Take the hand of the person sitting next to you,' said people all round the vast circle.

For just a moment Tamate was James Chalmers once again and his mind was on the other side of the world, in Scotland. Then he looked around at the laughter-filled faces of the villagers and thanked God that he'd been brought all the way from Scotland to Papua New Guinea. It took a little while for the party to settle down after all the hilarity, but when it did Tamate, through a translator, told the whole village about Jesus.

'It's going to rain before we reach our destination,' Tamate said, as he was leaving one village.

Dark clouds that had gathered around the hilltops were making their wet way down to a lower level.

'It will not rain,' a woman argued. 'The rainmaker is the only one who can make it rain and he has not done so.'

'What's the rainmaker's name and where is he?' the missionary asked.

'There he is,' the woman pointed. 'And his name is Kone.'

Tamate went over to Kone and talked with him.

'It is safe to go on,' the rainmaker said. 'I have not told it to rain so it won't. In fact, I will come with you to protect you from the rain coming on.'

As they walked through the forest Kone told them all about his amazing powers.

'Only the living God can send rain,' Tamate said. And as they walked the talk was all about Jesus.

'I feel drops of rain,' announced the missionary, as a storm began.

'Stop that!' Kone shouted. 'Rain, stay up there in the mountains!'

'It won't stop,' Tamate told him. 'God is sending the rain.'

The drops turned to a heavy shower then the heavy shower became torrential rain.

'You have more power than I have,' said Kone, upset and disappointed with himself.

'No,' said the missionary. 'I cannot make rain. Only God who made the heavens and the earth can make rain fall or stop it from falling.'

From then on Tamate and Kone were friends.

Sometimes the only way the Gospel could be taken to a village was by giving gifts to the villagers. Although Tamate would never give gifts to those who were armed with weapons to kill him, he did give things that made others raise their eyebrows.

'I need more gifts for the villagers,' he wrote to his mission on one occasion. 'Please send me a gross (144) of tomahawks and a gross of butcher's knives.' Of course, these were not given to kill humans but to kill animals for the cooking pot!

Some time after their first meeting, Tamate planned to set up a mission centre in the rainmaker's village.

'I will give you a piece of land to build on,' Kone said, and that's what he did.

The work went well until one day the villagers seemed unwilling to help with the building.

'What's wrong?' asked Tamate.

'It's bad news,' he was told. 'A warrior tribe is planning to raid us. Could you frighten them away with your guns please?'

'We can't do that,' the missionary explained. 'We are men of peace. Our guns are for hunting for food. We cannot set out to frighten people then tell them that we come in peace.'

As night drew in the women took everything that was precious to them and hid in the forest. An ominous silence filled the air.

'It's almost as though everyone is holding their breath waiting for the raid to begin,' said Tamate.

There was little sleep for anyone that night.

'They're here!' yelled the chief's wife in the dark hours of early morning. Her voice was filled with terror.

Tamate strode into the centre of the village where he found his friend.

'They know you're here,' Kone said. 'And they plan to kill you first.'

The darkness all around filled with screams of terror and pain and grief, and when morning light came there were horrible things to be seen.

'Peace!' shouted Tamate from the midst of the mayhem. 'Peace!'

The raiders stopped their evil work and looked at the strange white man.

'Give me that! And that! And that!' demanded Tamate, grabbing one spear then another from the warriors on both sides of the battle. Amazement was written all over their faces!

After much talking an uneasy peace reigned and the peacemaker walked back up the hill.

'Tamate!' a voice yelled behind him.

'They're going to kill Kone!'

Rushing down the hill into the thick of what had become another battle, the white man found himself surrounded. The leader of the raiders looked him in the eye, cruelty almost oozing from him.

'Go up the hill!' he said fiercely. 'We will not come up and you must not come down and interfere in our battle.'

'I will leave the village if there's going to be war,' Tamate said. 'I cannot preach Jesus among flying spears.'

After a long and noisy discussion peace was declared.

On his next visit to the area Tamate went to look for his friend.

'Where's Kone?' he asked.

The villager looked away.

'What's happened to Kone?'

Turning sadly to Tamate the villager told him that Kone was dead.

'Dead? What happened? Was he sick?'

The man shook his head then explained.

'There was another raid on the village. The warriors were determined to kill one man in particular. When a spear was thrown at him Kone jumped between the spear and the man it was aimed at. The spear hit Kone. The other man escaped.'

That night Tamate sat down to write his journal with a very heavy heart. And the words he wrote are these: 'My poor Kone! The kindest savage I have ever met. How anxious he was to be taught and to know how to pray! I taught him to say, "God of love, give me light; lead me to Christ." Who will deny that my rainmaking friend has passed from the darkness into the light that he prayed for.'

Snowballs at sea

'Who am I?' wondered Tamate, as the Australian boat steamed up the River Thames into the Port of London, England, in August 1886. 'When I left my friends at Port Moresby I was Tamate, their missionary and friend. Here I suppose I'm back to being James Chalmers. I wonder if I'll remember to answer to my own name!'

He stood on deck and looked at the buildings on either side of the river. It all seemed so unfamiliar, almost unreal. Mountains were what he wanted to see, wooded mountains towering 12,000 feet into the air. The dome of St Paul's Cathedral seemed so low and so tame compared to what he had left behind in Papua New Guinea.

'It won't be long until I'm back again,' he thought, and the thought cheered him up.

'Thank you for inviting me to speak about my work,' James said to the members of the Board of the London Missionary Society and others who had joined them for the occasion. 'Let me set the scene for you.'

Within minutes the men were transported in their minds to the land he loved. They felt the thrill of meeting the mission teachers, the fear of being chased by wild pigs and even wilder men, the horror of cannibalism, the heady clarity of the mountains and the steady rumble of surf on the many shores of which he spoke.

'The work is growing fast,' he concluded. 'We want

more men to work there, to take up the opportunities that are open. We NEED more men. That's why I've come home on this trip. It's to tell you that you MUST send more men out. We need missionaries in Papua New Guinea.'

'You're getting quite a reputation for yourself,' a friend told him when they met again for the first time since leaving Cheshunt College. 'I've heard you described as a bronzed savage, and the other day someone called you The Apostle of the Papuan Gulf. I was almost nervous of meeting you as you'd suddenly become so famous! I didn't know what I'd do with you.'

James grinned. 'I tell you what I'd like to do while we're here in London. I'd like to ride through the city on a horse-drawn cab!'

His friend laughed aloud. 'Really!' he said. 'You may have become famous but you're still the fun-loving James Chalmers I remember from twenty years ago!'

'Will you come and speak at our missionary meeting?'

'We've heard about your explorations and would like you to come and tell our geographical society about Papua New Guinea.'

'The members of our church have been praying for you since you went out to Rarotonga and we would very much like you to come and tell us how our prayers have been answered.'

Invitation after invitation arrived in James's mail and he said yes to as many of them as he could. His heart was on the other side of the world and his hope was that some of the people who heard him speaking would feel the Lord leading them to join in the work he was doing. Travelling was never a problem to the well-travelled missionary, and he certainly did more than his fair share of travelling during his time back in Britain.

'Well, well,' he smiled, as he thought about one invitation in particular. 'Who would ever have thought that James Chalmers, formerly well known as a local mischief, would be invited to speak to a great crowd of people in Inveraray Castle, by agreement of the Duke of Argyll himself! How my father would have loved that had he still been alive.'

Eight hundred people gathered in the castle pavilion to hear what the 'local boy' had to say.

'You won't remember me,' a middle-aged man said, looking the missionary in the eye.

James studied the face, saw the still boy-like grin, and laughed aloud.

'Johnnie!' he said, slapping his old friend on the back. 'You're still alive! You should have drowned years ago!'

'And so I would have done if you'd not hauled me out the River Aray!'

'Are there any others here from our school days?' asked James.

'There's one especially wanting to see you,' Johnnie said, leading his friend through the crowd.

A heavily-built weather-beaten man saw them coming and walked over to meet them. James knew from his walk that he was a seaman.

'So you're still going on and on about God, I hear,' said the stranger.

There was something in the teasing tone that struck a familiar chord.

'It's never Dugald?' queried James.

'It is so!' the sailor laughed. 'The very same Dugald. And it's better than good to see you again though I've no doubt you'll be preaching at me before the end of the night.'

But Dugald was wrong. So many people wanted to speak to their famous visitor that James had no time to preach, which was probably why Dugald winked cheekily at him on his way out the door!

James Chalmers found his spirits rising as the time drew near to return to his work, partly because he knew he was not going to be alone for very much longer. During the time he was home in Britain he became engaged to Sarah Eliza Harrison, who was to travel out to Australia where they planned to be married.

'15th June 1887,' James thought, as he wakened up on the day he was due to leave England. 'In just a few hours the good ship *Orient* will leave Plymouth and I'll be off on the first leg of my long journey home. Yes,' he thought, 'Papua New Guinea really is my home now.'

Before the ship had been long at sea James was heavily involved with the passengers and crew. He kept a diary of the voyage and it seems to have been both busy and enjoyable.

'Sunday July 10th. The Captain took a service on board today and I preached at it.'

'July 12th. I was chairman at a concert this evening. To save a lot of silly speechifying I did everything myself, even thanking myself for being chairman.'

'July 15th. Went to comfort two men who are ill. Got

them some medicine to help then told them sea stories for over an hour. They soon forgot they were sick!'

'July 23rd. Went for a rest this afternoon but was wakened up with an invitation to join in a tug-of-war. We had four strong men on our side and the other side stood no chance of winning.'

'July 27th. A poor Irish family had only sixpence left after paying for their voyage to Australia. The priest and I did a collection for them. They now have enough for their needs.'

'August 2nd. There's a refrigerator room on the ship where everything's frozen. Went there with some of the young men and had a splendid snowball fight!'

Two days later the *Orient* arrived in Australia.

'It's so much quicker,' James thought, 'now that ships are steam-powered, compared to when Jeanie and I first went out in the sailing ship *John Williams*.'

'Your first few days are very busy,' the traveller was told on arrival in Australia. 'You're having lunch with the Governor of Victoria. Several meetings have been arranged at which you will speak. The local paper wants an interview with you and you're preaching at three services on Sunday, two on Tuesday and two on Wednesday.'

'Back to work,' James commented with a smile, when he saw what had been planned for him. But he didn't really feel at home until he returned to Papua New Guinea. He sighed with relief when he finally arrived. 'I'm home. Home!' Then he grinned. 'And I'm not James Chalmers any more. I'm Tamate! That feels so good.'

For some time he remained with Mr and Mrs Lawes in Port Moresby, and as they talked together their thoughts and plans turned westwards to Motumotu.

'Do you think it wise to work there?' Mr Lawes asked, 'considering what happened last year.'

'In a way what happened gives all the more reason to work in Motumotu,' Tamate replied. 'It was a real tragedy that Tauraki was killed by the warriors. He was such a good teacher, one of my own 'boys' trained at Rarotonga. And it was so sad too that his colleague died of a fever soon afterwards. Both are home in heaven now but the work must go on. Those who killed Tauraki need to hear about Jesus.'

Despite all that had happened, Tamate was welcomed when he arrived in Motumotu.

'Look at that,' he said sadly to himself. 'The house that Tauraki and his family lived in is deserted and beginning to fall down. What a sad sight.'

Walking around the house, he saw a pile of timber already sawn into planks. Tamate stood and looked at the pile. 'I suppose Tauraki and the others did that,' he thought. Then a smile began to play on his face. 'That's what I'll do! There's enough wood here to build a house. It could become my base and from here I could reach out to all the villages round and about!'

'Aren't you afraid of the warriors who killed Taurake?' he was asked.

Tamate looked at the fearful Christian. 'No,' he said firmly. 'I'm not afraid of them.'

'And are you not afraid of the fevers that come from living in such a swampy place?'

'No,' said Tamate. 'If I've work to do here I've no reason to be afraid. God will keep me safe until the work is done. And when all my work on earth is done he'll take me home to heaven. Of what should I be afraid?'

Motumotu became Tamate's home. And it was to that home that he brought his second wife after their marriage in 1888.

'This isn't quite the welcome to our home that I'd planned,' said Tamate. 'The tide won't let us land at the village beach.'

'How will we get ashore?' Sarah asked.

'I'll walk through the water,' her husband smiled. 'But I think the villagers may have something more ladylike planned for you.'

They had.

A kind of stretcher was prepared for bearers to carry on their shoulders. First of all it was covered with a mat, then rough pillows stuffed with the silkiest of tree fibres were laid along its length to make it as comfortable as could be. The contraption was carried out to the boat and Sarah found herself being lifted gently on to it then borne on the shoulders of strong Motumotuans to their village home.

'I'm so tired,' thought Sarah, who had been ill on the way.

Seeing her weariness the village women prepared a makeshift bed while Tamate boiled water for cocoa.

'What an extraordinary place,' thought Sarah, when she wakened in the morning and looked around. 'The house is built on six feet high stilts! And the sea is so close that the roar of the surf is a constant background noise.'

'Do you like your specially designed furniture?' Tamate asked.

Sarah grinned. 'I do indeed,' she said. 'I've never before

had a washstand made of a bowl on an upside-down box. And none of my friends back in Britain have an old chest for a dressing table.'

'I imagine not!' Tamate laughed. 'And they probably have comfortable chairs rather than a home-made couch and some folding seats I bought in Australia.'

It was a poor home, but it was where Sarah wanted to be and she was happy.

'Hello,' said Sarah, to a woman who came to look at the white stranger.

Her visitor smiled and the two looked at each other. Sarah was dressed in a plain dark dress with a high neck and long sleeves. The Motumotuan women wore nothing at all apart from leaves, feather, shells and twine twisted from fine creepers!

Neither knew any words that the other understood but their smiles said what was in their hearts.

'I am glad to be here and it is good to meet you,' Sarah's smile told her visitor.

'Welcome to your new home,' the villager's smile said. 'And I would like to be your friend.'

'The girls have a hard life,' Sarah told her husband after a few weeks in Motumotu. From about the age of four they are really tiny working women. Even at four years old they babysit for their little brothers and sisters. They help with the cooking and I've even seen them out carrying bundles of wood nearly as big as themselves.'

'I know,' agreed Tamate. 'The boys have a much easier time.'

'I noticed that yesterday,' laughed Sarah. 'Some of

them were playing a very rowdy game, only one of the boys seemed much older than the others. And strangely, he looked like a Scot rather than a Motumotuan.'

'It was a really good game,' Tamate grinned. 'And you know that I've never really grown up.'

'It looked dangerous to me.'

'Not at all!' he explained. 'The boys divide into two groups. One group has spears and the other has coconuts. The ones with the coconuts stand at a safe distance when they throw them up in the air for the others to use for target practice.'

'I couldn't work out what happens when they miss them,' puzzled Sarah.

'Oh, that's simple,' said Tamate. 'If the spears don't hit the coconuts and they get through the 'enemy' line, the teams change over and they play again. It can go one for ages.'

Sarah looked at her husband and smiled. 'I noticed!'

Every Sunday Tamate held a service in the village, but often the only ones there were himself and his wife along with the missionary teachers and their wives.

'I'm going to try a change of tactics,' he told Sarah one Saturday evening. But he would say no more when she asked what he was going to do.

The following day there was only the usual little group of people at the service.

'Excuse me,' said Tamate, heading to the centre of the village.

'Look at that!' Sarah said, opened-eyed and nearly open-mouthed at her husband's antics.

He walked back and forth between the houses and each

time he came upon a little group of people he waved his arms in the air and shouted until they could ignore him no longer, and they were trying their hardest to ignore him!

'He's playing around until people are so curious they get up and follow him!' Sarah thought.

Round and round the houses he went, not caring a bit if he looked really stupid so long as men and women, boys and girls joined the little parade and followed him. Eventually he led them to where the service was to be held. Before anyone could escape, Tamate began to tell them such an interesting Bible story that they stayed and listened right to the end.

'Do you think the time has come to build a church?' Tamate asked one day.

'But we don't have any church members,' one of the missionary teachers pointed out.

Sarah smiled. She knew what her husband was thinking. *If we have a special building people are more likely to come, especially as they now trust us.*

Because they built it themselves, and used local materials, it didn't take long to put up the first village church in Motumotu.

'Let me tell you about it,' Sarah wrote home when the work was newly finished. 'The walls are made of the spines of nipa palm, and leaves have been thatched together to make the roof. It has six door spaces (without doors) two on each side and one at each end. That allows the air to move around and keep us cool but still keeps the rain off. The building also has windows. At least, it has square holes that look like windows but have no glass in them. And that's our church! When we had our first Communion service there was just the usual little group of us inside but villagers surrounded the church and listened to what was being said. And do you know what? It seemed as though they had all painted themselves especially brightly for the occasion!'

Crocodiles ahead!

'I would like to take a trip up to Moveave,' said Tamate when they were doing some future planning. 'And as you stayed here at Motumotu for nine weeks recently when I was visiting the Fly River area, I wondered if you would like to come with me this time.'

'Of course I would,' Sarah replied. 'But does that mean that you think it's nearly time to move on from here to Moveave?'

'No,' Tamate assured her. 'I think we still have work to do here before we leave it to the missionary teachers. I don't ever feel God wants me to move from a mission station until it's firmly established.'

'Have you been to Moveave before?' asked Sarah.

'Yes,' her husband frowned at the memory. 'And I'll never forget it. The people had a reputation for being a wild lot and it took hard work and much prayer to make some kind of peace with them. But you'll win over the womenfolk anyway. None of them have ever seen a white woman before and they'll treat you like a fragile china doll, not that they have any idea what a doll is, far less one made of fragile china!'

'As we're going on a larger boat than last time it'll take us longer to get there,' Tamate said, when they set out on their journey.

'Should it not be the other way round?' enquired Sarah.

'When we go by small boat or canoe we can travel along narrow creeks, and even move through stretches of swampy land between creeks. But using the larger boat means we have to stick to river travel and the rivers tend to meander rather than run in straight lines. But it means you'll see more of the country as we travel.'

'Crocodiles ahead!' one of the crew yelled.

'When I was a child at home I was sometimes taken out in a small rowing boat for a treat,' Sarah told one of the men on the boat. 'I used to trail my fingers in the water as we went. I loved the feel of the waves lapping.'

'Don't be tempted to do that here or you won't have any fingers left! You might not have any arms left either because crocodiles are hungry creatures.'

Sarah looked at the crocodiles in the water beside them.

'Some of them look like harmless rocks, almost like stepping-stones in the river, until you see their eyes,' she thought. Then a crocodile in the distance opened its mouth and snapped it shut. 'Goodness me!' she said. 'What strength! I'm sure he could bite off an arm right enough. I don't suppose a few fingers would do anything but take the edge of his appetite!'

'This is where we leave the boat,' Tamate explained. 'We'll visit this village then trek through the bush to Moveave.'

They were no sooner ashore than every woman and child in the village surrounded Sarah. So that she wasn't knocked over in the crush, her husband brought her a folding chair from the boat. Soon Sarah was presented with a drink of milk from a freshly cracked coconut.

'Thank you,' she said to the woman who gave it to her. 'It's lovely.'

Sarah had learned enough language to say these few words, but they set off an absolute torrent of speech from the people surrounding her as they thought she knew what they were saying! With much smiling and some other friendly expressions her husband had taught her, the white woman kept the crowd happy. And, as usual, where there was a crowd there was Tamate telling them about Jesus.

'I think we should move on now,' the missionary said, when he had spoken to the people and their chief. 'We'll come back here again.'

With his wife, his crewmen and his missionary teachers behind him, Tamate strode into the bush.

'I wonder if he ever thinks of the dangers of walking in the bush,' wondered Sarah, eyeing a snake curled round a branch not very far above her head. 'Or is he already thinking about what he'll do in Moveave.'

'Watch out!' said the teacher who was walking right behind her. 'See those large insects marching along there?'

Sarah nodded.

'They bite!'

Moving a little to the right of the path she passed the insects safely. 'They might bite,' she thought. 'But I've never seen such handsome insects before!'

'It's not far now,' Tamate called back. 'We'll be there within the hour.'

Sarah wasn't sorry. She was still getting into training for long treks through the bush!

'Why are those people fenced in?' she asked her husband as they reached the chief's house, Tamate's first port of call.

He realised immediately what had happened. 'I think the old chief has died,' he explained.

Still puzzled, Sarah took in the scene before her. Just in front of the chief's house was what looked like a tiny field, about nine feet, or two metres, square. In the field were an older woman, several younger men and women and a good number of children, all of them appearing as though they hadn't washed for ages!

'They look like a herd of poor neglected cattle waiting to be sold at a market!' she thought.

Tamate spoke quietly to the oldest of the young men in the enclosure for a long time. Then he took Sarah by the arm and introduced her to the old woman who was covered in what looked like lumps of clay. Some had dried off leaving just crumbs on her skin, others looked newer and stood out like swellings. She was the old chief's widow.

'This is my wife,' Tamate explained.

Sarah greeted the poor woman with a few words in her own language that brought the usual torrent of unintelligible reply. Tamate translated.

'She's telling you why they're cooped up like this,' he said. 'Her husband, the old chief, died and he's buried under this little compound. It's the tradition that the family now have to live in the field together. They cook here, and eat and sleep here as well. The only time they leave the little compound is to go into the bush when they need the toilet.'

His wife tried not to look surprised at what she was hearing because the widow was watching her face as Tamate translated the whole sad story.

130

'How long will they be cooped up like this?' she asked.

'That varies from village to village,' he explained. 'But it looks as though they've a little while to go yet.'

After a lengthy set of goodbyes Tamate and his companions moved down into the village itself, and they heard it before they saw it.

'What a difference,' thought Sarah. 'We've gone from a family in mourning to a village holding a feast!'

She looked around and took in the scene.

'There are people from other villages too,' she thought. 'They couldn't possibly all come from Moveave!' Sarah studied the houses on stilts between which they were passing, most with a platform at the front. 'Goodness me!' she said. 'Look at all that food!'

Above her head height, on the house platforms, were enough bundles of sago from the sago palms, yams and taro for a wedding feast, along with such big bunches of bananas that they needed two strong men to carry them! As the long welcoming ceremony continued Sarah looked longingly at the platforms covered with food. It was not that she was hungry, just that the fruit was in the shade of the houses and she was steaming hot!

'Would you like to rest in the shade?' one of the missionary teachers asked, when he realised how hot she was.

'Yes please,' said Sarah gratefully and then immediately changed her mind.

The home-made ladders to the houses were so rickety she didn't think she could get up one!

'Don't worry,' the teacher said. 'I'll get some branches and put in extra rungs for you!'

He had hardly said it before the deed was done. Sarah, feeling as though she was taking her life in her hands, swayed on a creeper as she climbed up the ladder to the platform of a house. She knew what it would feel like when she got there and that was what gave her the courage to climb on. For just a few seconds the shade made the perspiration on her skin turn cold and she shivered.

'How I love the shiver I get when I'm really hot and move into the shade. It's like a cold shower of rain on a hot summer day. Delicious!'

Tamate climbed up to join her and they relaxed before he spoke to the villagers from the Bible.

Sitting in the shade might have made Sarah nod off after all her exertions of getting to Moveave, but she was far too interested in what was going on down underneath her.

'Bedong! Bedong!' rang through the air. Sarah knew the noise. It was a stone-headed club hitting a not quite ripe coconut. Someone was ready for another drink.

'What's the celebration?' she asked her husband.

Tamate shook his head. 'I've not worked that out yet,' he answered. 'No doubt we'll find out after they've finished eating and all the welcoming ceremonies are over.'

'Pyoing!'

'What's that?' demanded Tamate, jumping to his feet and making the house platform shudder.

'It's an arrow! Get into the house!'

Sarah moved from the shade of the platform back into the house and looked out. Not Tamate! He was down the ladder in a flash.

'Pyoing!' came from the left, and his quick eyes searched in that direction for the person who had shot it.

'Pyoing!'

This time it was from the right.

'What's going on?' he demanded.

'Pyoinnng! Thud!' One landed hear his feet in the ground. He looked down at the still quivering arrow.

'Pyoing!'

'Pyoing!'

'Pssshewww!' A spear flew though the air above his head. Tamate could feel the air ripple as it passed!

He stared around at the mayhem where a party had been five minutes before! A young man, his face contorted with rage, poised to throw his spear. Tamate looked in the direction of throw and yelled out a warning.

'Duck!'

Boys, too small to be warriors, raced around the men, annoying them into even more ferocity.

'Get him!

'Shoot the arrows further!

'Thump that one!'

'Help! He hit me!'

'This is utterly ridiculous!' thought Tamate, practical as ever and apparently unfazed by the battle going on all around him.

Sarah watched through a crack in the wall and saw what happened next.

'Stop fighting and tell me what this is all about!' Tamate shouted above the din.

It took several minutes, but there was something about the white man standing unafraid in the middle of the rumpus that made the men sheath their arrows and lay down their clubs and spears. Even the pesky boys stopped and looked at Tamate.

'Now,' the missionary said firmly, like an old-fashioned

headmaster, 'what started off that stupid behaviour?'

Several of the men spoke at once, quietly at first then louder. In less time than it takes to tell, one of the best shots had an arrow primed in his bow ready to start the battle all over again!

'Stop!' yelled Tamate. 'Speak one at a time and tell me what this is all about.'

Eventually the story came out. There had been a disagreement between a villager and one of his own mission teachers! It was the kind of thing that would have been settled with just a few sharp words in most places. Not in Papua New Guinea!

Sarah, who had spent the time watching what was happening and praying that God would prevent anyone being killed, looked at her husband in astonishment.

'How does he do that?' she asked, for it wasn't the first time she'd seen his commanding performance. 'God has given him a gift for stopping fights becoming open warfare.'

She knew, as Tamate and his companions knew, that had that battle not been stopped before the village men got to the stage of really enjoying themselves, none of them would have got out of Moveave alive. Not only would the old chief have been buried near the village, but Tamate, Sarah, their teachers and the other men who had come with them would all have been buried there too.

'Or not!' she thought suddenly, remembering that there were still many villages in Papua New Guinea where cannibalism was not unknown.

While Sarah's life was sometimes in danger when she went trekking with Tamate, there were times when it was also in danger when she was left behind at home!

'It's three weeks since I last wrote in my diary,' she scribbled with an unsteady hand. 'I've had such a time. While Tamate was away I developed a high fever and was so ill I thought I would die. There was nobody who knew anything about medicine within reach, and the more ill I became the more difficult I found it to remember any of the local language. I knew I needed some drops of aconite to save my life, and I knew I needed them quickly. But how to get them? The aconite was in the store with all the other medicines and I could as easily have walked a million miles as walked the few feet to the store.'

Sarah stopped writing. She was still very weak.

'Are you telling the whole sad story to your diary?' asked Tamate, who had been home just a few days.

Sarah shook her head. 'I'm telling the whole wonderful story to my diary,' she corrected, lifting up her pen again.

'One day, when I was at my very worst,' she continued, 'some men actually carried me from our home into the store and right up to the medicine shelf. They then touched the medicine bottles one by one to find out which would help me. I shook my head at each of the wrong ones and just had the strength to nod when one of the good men touched the aconite. But how was I going to administer a few drops? I used sign language to get the men to hold me by the elbows to let me count out the drops of aconite. Then, after I had taken it, they tenderly carried me back to my bed and laid me down to sleep ... or to die.'

Sarah looked up and could picture the scene. How wonderfully patient these men had been!

'When I awoke,' she wrote, 'I was less fevered and I realised that I would live. It was the men who helped me till then, but the women now tried to do what they could.

One made me a watery porridge, but it had stuck to the bottom of the pan and was too burnt to eat. Poor woman, it was so kind of her to try to make something I could eat! Then another baked some bread but I wasn't well enough to eat it. What they did do that really helped me was to make me tea, tea, more tea, and even more tea. Between tea and some other drinks I managed to survive for the next ten days. I was so glad to see Tamate arrive back home because at one stage I thought he'd return to find my freshly covered grave! How good God is!'

Over the months that followed Tamate realised that the work at Motumotu was well established. Was God showing him that the time had come to leave the little church, the village and the people in the care of some missionary teachers? And, if it had, where did God mean him to go next? In his heart Tamate already knew the answers to his questions. Yes, Motumotu was established. Yes, the mission teachers would be able to look after the work. And ... he felt sure he should move to the Fly River.

'But what about Sarah?' he wondered. 'She's been so poorly. She really needs a break before coming to the Fly River. If she were to go back to Britain for a visit I could find the right village and have a house built for her return.'

'I know it's for the best,' Sarah agreed, when they discussed the issue. 'But I really don't want to go.'

Tamate knew exactly how she felt because he felt just the same.

'March 1982. How I dread this parting,' wrote Sarah. 'I know that months may elapse before I get any letters from Tamate. Sickness or death may take either one of us. What a comfort it is to know that everything is in God's hands and all that he does is good.'

Stone gods and clubs

It was over two years before Tamate and Sarah met again, and their reunion took place on English soil. On his last visit to Britain the missionary had spent the time wishing himself back in Papua New Guinea, this time he was just glad to be reunited with his wife!

'So many people want you to speak at meetings,' Sarah said. 'But you'll have to be careful. You're tired out after years of hard work and you're needing a break.'

'Wives!' laughed Tamate. 'How they nanny their poor husbands!'

But despite making a joke of it, he knew he needed time to recover from all his extraordinary experiences. However, being back in Britain brought new experiences too.

'August is just the wrong time to visit Inveraray,' laughed Tamate.

Even in Britain James Chalmers was now known as Tamate. Although it was a great surprise to him, he found that he was really quite famous!

'What's wrong with August?' a friend asked. 'I would have thought that Scotland would be lovely then.'

'So it is,' Tamate explained. 'But the midges like August too and they can make life an absolute misery!'

'Surely you're used to all sorts of biting insects in Motumotu,' observed his friend.

'I know,' agreed the missionary. 'But you've never met the Argyllshire variety of the Scottish midge!'

The visit to Inveraray in August 1895 was to celebrate a most special occasion. Tamate was to be made a Freeman of the Burgh of Inveraray. This is the highest honour that can be awarded by a Scottish town or city.

'I thought it was only in Papua New Guinea that it could rain like this!' Sarah commented, as she looked out the window.

Tamate smiled. 'There's a special kind of rain falls in Inveraray,' he teased. 'We call it forgetful rain.'

His wife looked puzzled. 'Why's that?'

'Well,' he said, 'sometimes when it rains it forgets that it has ever rained before and just keeps coming as though making up for lost time!'

On the day of the presentation the rain was forgetful, it forgot to rain altogether, and the crowd that gathered arrived dry in Inveraray Courthouse for the ceremony.

'I award Mr James Chalmers the Freedom of the Burgh of Inveraray in recognition of his career as a missionary and his eminent services in the cause of civilization and the spread of the Gospel,' the Provost said, as he presented Tamate with a silver casket bearing the burgh seal.

The new Freeman looked round the Courthouse at friends of long ago.

'I've had many honours in my time,' Tamate said. 'I've been initiated into the tribes of Papua New Guinea and received by them as a brother. When I was home nine years ago the Royal Geographical Society presented me with their diploma, because of the exploring I've done, though I'm a missionary rather than an explorer. But this honour, the Freedom of my own Royal Burgh of Inveraray, means something very special to me.'

When the local newspaper came out the following week it carried a report of the occasion and remembered back to before James was famous, to when he was just well-known as a young rogue at home!

'It might interest the younger people of the town to know that he was a member of the first cricket club established in this part of the Highlands, and he was considered a first-class football player in the district. Indeed, there were few things, bad or good, that took place in Inveraray that he did not have something to do with.'

There were not many people in Inveraray more delighted that day than Mr Meikle.

'What a boy he was!' the minister remembered. 'He could have gone either way because of the mischief in him. How good God has been to take the energy that used to get him into trouble and channel it into a wonderful work.'

The following Sunday Tamate spoke at his old Sunday School.

'You might recognise this young man,' said Mr Meikle, when he introduced a boy to the visitor. 'He's as like his father as can be.'

Tamate looked at the lad and his mind zipped back over the years. This boy was amazingly like the young lad James had dragged out the River Aray!

'Johnnie's boy!' Tamate exclaimed.

'My dad says you and he got into trouble sometimes,' another curly-haired boy said, when they were introduced.

Having looked at the teenager for a long moment Tamate smiled. 'You're sure to be Calum's son!'

The boy grinned in agreement.

'Did he ever tell you the story about the grunting-wheezes?' asked the missionary.

Mr Meikle looked very puzzled.

Tamate told the Sunday School boys about the night he and his friends decided to disrupt the meeting in the joiner's loft in the Maltland, and about how that was the very night when he was challenged to become a Christian. Before he finished his talk, Tamate appealed to the boys to think about their futures and to ask themselves if God might be calling them to serve him in some faraway place.

On 13th November 1895, Tamate left England once again and headed for Papua New Guinea. Transport had progressed so much over the years that he arrived home just two months and a week later, on 20th January 1986.

'I think we should move our headquarters to Saguane and build up the work there,' he said to Maru, one of his mission teachers.

Maru was also a carpenter and he knew exactly what to do. He dismantled the building they were in and arranged for it to be taken plank by plank, stilt by stilt, to Saguane!

'There's more building to be done,' Tamate said, when they'd begun to settle in their new centre. 'I know there are only a few children having lessons here but the numbers will grow and we'll need some kind of building for a school.

Maru looked up at the heavy clouds in the sky.

'Yes,' he agreed. 'We have so much rain here that we can't expect the children to be taught outside.'

Tamate laughed. 'Not unless we're willing to risk some of them being washed away.'

There was a pause as he thought for a moment. 'Actually,' he said jokingly, 'I can think of a few of them that I wouldn't mind being washed away. They're such scamps!'

When Sarah arrived at Saguane she looked around at her new home.

'We're right among the swamps here,' she thought. 'No wonder the children look poorly. I don't think we can be more than twelve feet above sea level!'

Tamate began to tell his wife a little more about her new home. 'The number coming for lessons has lurched between two and fifteen, but it's beginning to settle at twelve to fifteen. Keeping them still is a problem. Their eyes are everywhere! Their tongues never stop and their feet want to be on the run all the time.'

'They're boys,' Sarah smiled. 'And I think boys can all be defined as movement and noise with dirt on!'

With a great deal of work school attendance rose to over thirty and Manu, with the help of the villagers, built a schoolroom and a simple house for boys who came from distant villages and were unable to go home each night.

Every day Tamate held a service in Saguane. At first people walked past suspiciously, but over time some came and listened to what he had to say.

'Some people want to be baptised,' a helper told him.

The missionary was pleased to hear that, but a little concerned at the same time.

'I'm not sure if they're really Christians yet,' he answered. 'And they need to be truly forgiven and seriously trying to follow Jesus before they can be baptised.'

'But some of them even pray at the service,' insisted his colleague.

That day Tamate carefully translated the chief's prayer

from the local language into English. It suggested that perhaps the man had a little way to go before baptism.

'Lord God,' he prayed, 'we much want tobacco and cloth, tomahawks and knives!'

'There's an annual snake festival held here,' Tamate explained to his wife. 'That's what all the excitement's about.'

'What does it involve?' asked Sarah.

The missionary shook his head. 'It's awful, worse than any other heathen festival I've ever come across. People trek from a huge area to it and it always ends in murder and mayhem. In the last few years I understand that there have been many murders, not to say other terrible things being done to people.'

'It was bad for the mission teacher last time,' Manu remembered. 'When so many people died the chiefs held a meeting and decided that it was because some of the villagers were listening to what the teacher was telling them about Jesus! Apparently nobody came to the services for a long time afterwards.'

'That's right,' agreed Tamate. 'But when I next visited the village I told them what I thought of that idea! People trickled back after that, but it took some courage.'

Sarah looked thoughtful. 'At home in Britain when people become Christians the worst that usually happens to them is that their families and friends laugh at them. It's so different here. Showing an interest in Jesus can mean a stone club hitting the back of your head or a spear right through you.'

That was not the only time Tamate met the power of fear that came from the worship of spirit gods.

'18th December 1896,' he wrote in his diary, then sat back to think how to describe his most recent adventure. 'I'm just back from a ten-week trek round the mission stations. What an adventure we had at sea! After we left one place the seas and current drove us on to a sandbar. It looked as though the ship would break up under the strain. The anchor was no use at all. In fact, it was dangerous to use it. Orders were given to slack out every inch of chain so letting the seas drive the boat over the sandbar and through the outer line of breakers. The sea smashed and crashed on deck as we worked.'

Tamate frowned. It wasn't the memory of the storm that made him frown, but what happened next.

'Some villagers on shore saw our danger and paddled out in their canoes to rescue us and take us to land. The next day we went back out to the boat and with the help of about a hundred men we lightened the load on the ship then floated her off the sandbar before reloading her cargo. It was quite an operation.'

He shook his head as he continued to write.

'While they were moving the cargo the men discovered some stone gods on the ship. They decided they were the ancestors of their own gods and that's why we'd nearly all been drowned. The truth is that they're just lumps of carved stone! It was a tricky situation!'

As the work at Saguane progressed, and the little group of Christians became stronger in their faith, Tamate spent more time in other villages. He tried to place a mission teacher in each one, either a Papua New Guinean Christian or someone from one of the other South Sea Islands.

Although most were reliable and worked very hard, that was not always the case.

'What have you been doing?' Tamate asked, when he revisited the teacher in Mabuiag. 'I asked you to prepare for a church by finding good wood and cutting it into planks ready for building. But now I find you already have a building!'

The man didn't seem to know whether to look proud or sorry.

'I asked the people for help over and over again until they gave me wood and then I built the church,' he explained, looking at his feet rather than at Tamate.

Shaking his head, the missionary stared sadly at the shoddy church that would fall down before too many storms hit it.

'I explained to you that the people here are poor, that they're going through a famine, and that they need all their time and effort to find food to keep them alive! And you took them away from that to find wood for a church! No wonder they cut down any old trees, whether they were suitable or not. The poor people!'

Struggling to be patient, Tamate asked about the school the teacher was meant to run. The man continued to look at his feet.

'I've not been teaching for a while,' he admitted. 'I was too busy building the church and doing other things.'

'So it was more important to do what I told you not to do than to do what you were asked to do?' thought Tamate.

'We'll have a serious talk later,' was all he said.

Things were not all gloomy. In fact, the missionaries had much to be thankful for.

'It's amazing,' said Sarah, when her husband returned from a trek. 'The children are learning even though their behaviour is "unusual." If anything goes wrong they fight tooth and nail, usually tooth. Sometimes, when I hear screams and yells that make me wonder if someone is being murdered, I discover teeth marks on several of the little monsters! Then I remember that many of them come to school despite their parents wanting to keep them away. And as long as they come to school they hear about the Lord Jesus. That makes it all worthwhile.'

She looked at her husband who was smiling at her stories of what had happened while he was away.

'He really loves these people,' she thought. 'His eyes light up when a new person comes to church. And it doesn't matter how dirty or smelly or horribly painted they are, even if he knows they've murdered during tribal wars he welcomes them in.'

Numbers attending both school and church rose over time, and each new arrival brought a smile to Tamate's face. So much happened in November 1898 that he sat down and listed the good things for which he had to thank God.

'Last month I baptised sixty-four people at Parama and thirty-two at Geavi, as well as many of the new Christians' children. Then I baptised fourteen here at Saguane and seven children. Not only that, but the average attendance at school is now fifty-three! God's making so much happen that I really need a good and reliable helper.'

Sarah Chalmers also had numbers on her mind at New Year 1900. Each New Year was celebrated with special services to which many people came from all around.

'Are you all right?' Tamate asked, when he saw his exhausted-looking wife in the crowd.

'I'll keep going as long as I have to,' she said, trying to look energetic. 'But I think I'll go to bed for the whole month of January!'

'I estimate we have about 1,700 people here,' announced her husband. 'And some came too early and had to leave before the festival really began.'

'No doubt others will come after it's all over too,' laughed Sarah. 'They always do.'

'Look at them!' Tamate laughed. 'I just love seeing them enjoying sports. To think that they find ordinary races fun when their best idea of fun used to be racing to spear someone or thump a stone-headed club down on the back of an unsuspecting skull.'

Suddenly his face became serious.

'How much we have to thank God for,' he said. 'And not just that the people are here having fun without killing each other. But yesterday 300 people were at our Communion service. And over 130 adults have asked for baptism after the open air service later this week!'

'That's what we came for,' thought Sarah. 'We came to tell people about Jesus and hundreds have come to believe in him.'

She was so full of joy that she forgot for a while about her poor tired body.

Three months later there was joy once again in Tamate's home for the helper for whom he had prayed came at last. He was so pleased with Oliver Tomkins that he wrote to his mission and asked them to send another two the same!

'You'll never guess what this is!' laughed Tamate, as he unpacked a wooden crate that arrived by boat soon afterwards.

Sarah looked at the package her husband removed from the crate. It was a very odd shape and her guesses were wildly wrong.

Producing a church bell like a great rabbit out of a huge hat, Tamate grinned from ear to ear.

'Long ago, when I was a Glasgow City Missionary, I was told never to forget Inveraray. And I never have. The amazing thing is that Inveraray has never forgotten me. The letter that came with the package says that this is the bell of Mr Meikle's church and they have sent it out for us to use here. It's a little bit of Scotland that will remain in Papua New Guinea long after we've gone.'

It was a great thrill to Tamate to hang the bell and use it to call the children to school for their lessons and to call the people to church to worship God.

That spring it became clear that Sarah's tiredness was more than just overwork. Although she continued to teach for as long as she could, by the end of July she was ill in bed and she was never again able to rise without help.

'Peace, perfect peace,' Sarah was heard to say, even when she was terribly ill.

And there were few things she enjoyed better than hearing the school children singing outside her home.

'What little mischiefs they are,' she thought, as she lay listening to them. 'But how I love them.'

'I'm going to take the service now,' Tamate told her one day. 'Are you all right on your own.'

Sarah smiled and said, 'Jesus is near, very near.'

147

And on 25th October 1900 she died and went to heaven to be with her Lord Jesus Christ for ever more.

Nearly six months later Tamate and Oliver Tomkins set out to visit the people of Goaribari Island.

'Look at this,' said Oliver. 'There's a welcome party making its way out to meet us.'

Tamate looked towards the island. 'Their canoes are lying low in the water,' he said.

Travelling with the two missionaries was Hiro, a teacher from Rarotonga, the chief of the Ipisia people and ten mission boys.

'That's because they're armed fit to fight a war!' said Hiro. 'Look! Their canoes are stuffed with clubs, spears, knives, stones and weapons of all sorts.'

The first of the canoes reached their boat very quickly and the islanders swarmed on board.

'Come and visit us,' they said. 'Come to our village and meet us.'

Tamate looked at the afternoon sun sinking and said that it was far too late. They would row over to the island in the morning. The islanders took a lot of persuading to leave the ship, but eventually they did so and paddled their weapons back home to the village for the night.

'Good morning,' said Oliver Tomkins, when they met first thing the next day. 'I see our visitors are coming to escort us ashore.'

Canoes drew alongside and the ship swarmed with people wanting Tamate and his companions to visit their village.

'Let's go ashore before breakfast,' said Tamate. 'I don't

think we'd have peace to eat it anyway!'

Setting off in their whaleboat, the two missionaries and the others who went with them arrived to an enthusiastic welcome. As soon as they reached the beach Goaribari islanders surrounded them.

'Come into our hut,' said the men. 'Come and see what we have prepared for you.'

The visitors were led into the huge village hut where Tamate immediately recognised the last-minute preparations for a cannibal feast. Painted islanders, each wielding a stone-headed club, slunk behind their visitors. Tamate, Oliver Tomkins and their Christian friends knew little of what happened next. All they knew was that they were safe home in heaven and saw Jesus face to face.

Life Summary: James Chalmers

James Chalmers was the son of a Scottish stonemason who was based in the town of Inveraray. His parents were Christians and his father never missed a church service if he could help it.

In James's early teens, his pastor read a letter from a missionary in Fiji and asked the question, 'I wonder if there is a boy here this afternoon who will yet become a missionary, and by and by bring the Gospel to the cannibals?' James felt a call from God to mission and thought to himself, 'Yes, God helping me, I will.' However James had no real interest in God. But this changed after attending a revival meeting in the town. His intention was to go there and make trouble with some other lads, but a friend urged him to go to the meeting to hear what was being said. The message of Revelation 22:17 brought James to a knowledge of his own need of salvation.

James at once began to help out at public meetings in the town. After eight months working with Glasgow City Mission, and some further education, he went on to study Rarotongan, a language that he would later use in his missionary work in the South Sea Islands.

James married Jeanie Hercus on October 17, 1865. Two days after their wedding Chalmers was ordained. And on January 4, 1866, the young couple set sail for the South Pacific on board the *John Williams*.

Despite a shipwreck they arrived at their destination and James was the first to be carried ashore at Rarotonga. There were many natives there who longed to hear more of the good news of Jesus Christ, but there were others whose lives were greatly under the influence of alcohol. There were struggles and there were victories. Eventually Chalmers was called to New Guinea, a largely unexplored island where there were still some cannibals. Mrs Chalmers finally succumbed to poor health and was sent to Sydney for rest and recovery. She died there on February 20, 1879.

Chalmers coped with his grief by getting even more involved in the work of the mission field. As a pioneer he pressed on into the interior. In 1882 Chalmers was able to write that there were now 'no single cannibals, ovens, no feasts, no human flesh, no desire for skulls.' Tribal warfare decreased and James was even given heathen temples in which to preach. In 1888, after a visit to his home country, Sarah Eliza Harrison followed him out to the mission field and became his wife. In 1900, after fourteen weeks of severe sickness, Sarah also died.

On April 4, 1901, Chalmers visited the region of the Goaribari Island. On the evening of April 7, they anchored off the end of the island. Next morning Chalmers and his companions went ashore for an hour before breakfast. The boat waited all day but the missionaries did not return. James Chalmers and his friends were struck from behind with stone clubs, knocked to the ground and murdered.

Papua New Guinea Today

Papua New Guinea or PNG, occupies the eastern half of the island of New Guinea and numerous offshore islands. It is located in the southwestern Pacific Ocean. Its capital is Port Moresby. PNG has over 850 indigenous languages and at least as many traditional societies, out of a population of just over 5 million. Only 18 per cent of its people live in urban centres.

The country's geography is diverse and extremely rugged. A spine of mountains runs the length of the island. Dense rainforests can be found in the lowland and coastal areas. In some areas planes are the only method of transport. Papua New Guinea gained its independence from Australia in 1975.

The country is situated on the Pacific Ring of Fire, at the point of collision of several tectonic plates. Active volcanoes, eruptions and earthquakes are relatively frequent, sometimes accompanied by tsunamis.

Other major islands within Papua New Guinea include New Ireland, New Britain, and Bougainville.

Papua New Guinea is one of the few regions close to the equator that experience snowfall, which occurs in the most elevated parts of the mainland.

Official languages: English; Tok Pisin; Hiri Motu
Area: 462, 840 Km^2
Highest peak: Mount Wilhelm at 4,509 m; 14,793 ft
Population: (July 2005) 5, 887, 000
Currency: Kina

James Chalmers: Maps

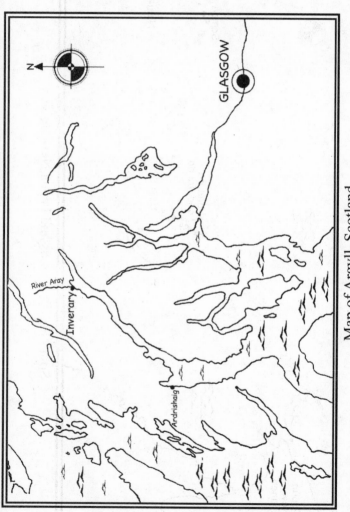

Map of Argyll, Scotland

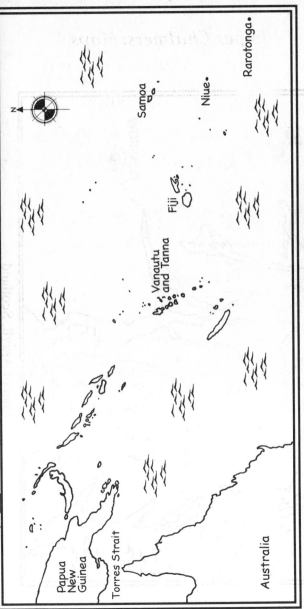

South Pacific Islands and Papua New Guinea

James Chalmers Timeline

1841	**James Chalmers born in Ardrishaig, Argyllshire, Scotland.**
	First full census in Britain in which all names were recorded.
1843	First public telegraph line, from Paddington to Slough.
	Dickens' *A Christmas Carol* was published.
1844	First Morse message transmitted in the USA (Baltimore to Washington).
1846	An anaesthetic used for the first time in England.
1848-9	**Chalmers Family moved to Glengary, Scotland.**
	California gold rush.
1851	**Chalmers rescued a schoolmate from drowning.**
1855	Florence Nightingale introduced hygiene into military hospitals in Crimea.
	Livingstone found the Victoria Falls.
1856	**Chalmers heard a letter read in Sunday-school, resolved to be a missionary.**
1859	**Chalmers converted in a November revival meeting in Inveraray.**
1861	American Civil War began.
1862	**Chalmers entered Cheshunt College.**
1864	**Chalmers entered London Missionary Society College at Highgate.**
1865	**Chalmers married Miss Jeanie Hercus. Ordained in Finchly Chapel.**
	End of American Civil War – slavery abolished in USA.
1866	**Chalmers sailed from England January 4.**
1867	**James Chalmers arrived at Rarotonga.**

1876	Alexander Graham Bell invented telephone. Victoria proclaimed Empress of India.
1877	**Chalmers left for Port Moresby.**
1879	**Mrs Jeanie Chalmers died at Sydney, Australia, February 20.**
1886	**Chalmers on furlough May 11 to September, 1887.**
1888	**Chalmers married to Sarah Eliza Harrison in Cooktown.**
1890	London's first electric Underground.
1894	**James Chalmers on furlough May to January 20, 1896.**
1899	Aspirin invented.
1900	**Second Mrs Chalmers died, October 25.**
1901	**James Chalmers killed and eaten by cannibals.** Commonwealth of Australia founded. Queen Victoria died – Edward VII crowned king.

CHRISTIAN FOCUS PUBLICATIONS

Christian Christian   CF4K   Mentor
Focus   Heritage

Christian Focus Publications publishes books for adults and children under its four main imprints: Christian Focus, Christian Heritage, Christian Focus 4 Kids and Mentor. Our books reflect that God's word is reliable and Jesus is the way to know him, and live for ever with him.

Our children's publication list includes a Sunday school curriculum that covers pre-school to early teens; and puzzle and activity books. We also publish personal and family devotional titles, biographies and inspirational stories that children will love.

If you are looking for quality Bible teaching for children then we have an excellent range of Bible story and age specific theological books.

From pre-school to teenage fiction, we have it covered!

Find us at our web page:
www.christianfocus.com

CF4·K
*Because you're never
too young to know Jesus*